The Links of Evalon

A novel by

Zachary Michael Jack

SWC PRESS

Sportswriters Collaborative

Chicago ⋏ Oxford

Sportswriters Collaborative
27 North Wacker Drive
Chicago, IL 60606

ISBN 978-0-9845083-0-3
Library of Congress Control Number 2010903659

Illustrations © 2010 Celeste Pille
Cover images ©iStockphoto.com

For my father

The Links of Evalon

STRAIGHT
SHOOTER

One

When my son slugged me on the golf course I'd gritted my teeth and said, *Pack your bags, sport. We're going to Grum's cabin.* He'd nodded, grimly, like he'd been expecting it.

We'd been paired with two oldsters when the kid reared back and sucker punched me. One of the old dudes had laid his mitt on my collarbone as I'd tried to catch my breath and said, *Jack, why'd your boy do that?*

Long ago, about the time I'd started to become a know-it-all teen like Drew, my own father had begun traveling out West each winter for what he called a "retreat." He'd said he needed a break from his lawyering, but really I think he needed a break from his snot-nosed kid…me.

He'd always dreamed of playing Pebble Beach, so when he'd arrived to find the famous links storm-closed, he'd wandered further south, to the sleepy fishing villages and rugged mountain ranges mid-coast, in search of the next best thing.

Shortly thereafter, he'd written Mom and me an enthused postcard telling us he'd been directed to a guy named Grum, an old shepherd with a cabin to let. He had a good feeling about it, he'd said.

From that day forward, Dad ended up returning to Grum's every winter for the rest of his life. Grum treated him like a son, Grum's own son, Peter, having long since flown the coop for the old country, South Africa, where apparently Grums were as thick as thieves. In any case, the elder Grum came to think highly enough of my old man to make him heir to the little cabin that adjoined his "Big House." And Dad, when his time came, passed the dump on to me.

My weeks there until that fall of my thirteenth year felt like they'd never end. No indoor plumbing, no TV, no girls, no nothing. Dad would go practically mute, spending long hours writing, drawing, humming to himself—breathing in the peace he could never seem to find back home. Then in the afternoon, when he was ready, it was understood I would walk with him on the cliffs overlooking the Pacific. He would stroll with his hands clasped together behind his back the way ministers and philosophers do, and I would tag along behind him, on eggshells.

A year ago, in our divorce negotiations, Drew's mother had insisted I take Grum's cabin. In return, I'd tried to pawn it off on her. Peter Grum still jetted in from Johannesburg once or twice a year to check on the Big House he'd inherited, but otherwise the entire "estate," I'd been told, had pretty much gone to the raccoons. Still, our mediator pointed out, the land was priceless. She'd laughed out loud at our dispute, telling us we must be the first couple in history to try to force a piece of coastal property off on one another. Neither of us would budge. Finally, I'd agreed to assume the haunt if the wife would allow me to take Drew to the cabin, and for two draft picks to be named later.

I hadn't bothered to stop and think how much it would cost in time and treasure to bring the kid here. There'd been so much I'd needed to tell him—so much I'd stuffed away inside me thinking one day, when I had a man-cub of my own, I'd spill my guts about everything that'd happened to Dad and me on this magical coast.

Fatherhood hasn't happened the way I'd hoped. I came to it late in the game, afraid, I guess, that what befell me and my pop would befall me and Drew. I promised myself I'd be a cool dad, involved in my son's life, attuned to his every mood and feeling. But somehow, like giving in to gravity, my fatherhood assumed the same shape my old man's had in the years before we set foot on the Links of Evalon…hopelessly private, distant from a boy who was growing up before his very eyes, not because he'd wanted it that way, but because, not having a father of his own, he hadn't known how else to act.

Like falling victim to a swing flaw you thought you'd licked, like forgetting a name you should've long ago committed to memory—after a while it's the shame that quiets you.

In the days leading up to my and Drew's arrival here, in the months it took me to catch my breath after his sucker punch and his mom's socking it to me in divorce negotiations, I'd found myself looking at the kid as if he were an alien. He'd made me angry, reminding me of my own miserable failures as his father. I'd wanted to hug him and give him every ounce of love and wonder I'd ever experienced, but something inside me—something I hated—stopped me cold.

Eva-what? Drew had looked at me like I was crazy when I'd broken the news I'd be pulling him out of school, and that I'd booked us flights to Grum's, just as my own father had a generation before, when we'd arrived on the coast in time to celebrate his 60th birthday together. The echoes between my own boyhood and Drew's had already begun to grow eerie.

Evalon. Something caught in my throat when I'd said the name of the island links to my son, my tongue wrapping around the word for the first time in decades, the word that'd changed my life, and my father's, forever.

And now here we are, a generation later, father and son, Jack and Drew Johannes—*Jack* and *Little Jack* people call us, we're

11

so much alike—in the same glum cabin, musty with decades of disuse, a fire slowly breathing life, coffee perking in the same kettle my father favored, fog rolling in thick as a mystery, Drew silently cursing what no doubt feels to him, as it did to me, like a punishment.

Tomorrow, he'll be forced to spend my 60th birthday with me on the same rocky coastline where, many moons ago, Grum and Dad and I hit celebratory shots into the sea in honor of the old man's 60 candles.

Because it's here and only here—at Grum's—that I can begin to tell him my story.

FATHER-SON
TOURNEY

Two

When I was a teenager I was crazy about golf, and I was good at it, too. We were never members anywhere … Dad said that wasn't the kind of people we were. Besides, he'd said, I had plenty of space to play at our house. We had acres before the land got subdivided.

Summers I'd disappear after breakfast and hit balls until suppertime. Dad, meanwhile, would spend his days in his study when he wasn't meeting with clients about their cases. Most nights, he'd find me before dinner and watch me hit a few dozen.

His arrival always made me nervous. I'd be alone all day hitting incredible shots, then when he'd come, I'd start messing up. When that happened, he'd gently take the club from my hand, and address the next pearl in the pile. He was a tall man, Dad was, taller than I am now, and he looked almost silly bending over a shot with my little, junior sticks.

He'd line up quickly, expertly, like he was hitting a 1-iron to seal the deal at the U.S. Open at Pebble. And then he'd swing, the ball hissing off the clubface. He'd smile ever so slightly as it came to rest a couple hundred yards out, click the toe of his wingtip with the clubhead, and hit another. Then he'd half-smile again, and hold the club out for me. That was his idea of instruction.

The funny thing is, it worked. I got better quickly, and though he grumbled about it, he allowed me to enter the junior opens at the country clubs around home. He'd drive me to the tournaments as long as I was willing to stay until dinnertime when he'd pick me up, always at six o'clock sharp, whether I'd finished my round at noon or at five. He'd pop the trunk, I'd throw the sticks in the back, and we'd ride home to break bread with mom while he whistled into the wind.

He never asked me how I played. I think sometimes if Dad sensed—and he always seemed to—whether I'd had an especially good or bad round he'd ask me about it, but that didn't happen very often.

He and I didn't play together on a course for at least a couple of years. I knew he would play on his own because he'd take his clubs from his study, load up the car, and be gone for hours. I begged him to play with me. But he always said the same thing—*Maybe when you're a little older.*

Then the father-son championship came along at the club where I'd won the junior open that year. I was automatically entered, and Dad along with me. Dad was well-known around town—any lawyer practicing in a burg the size of ours was, even if he took as few cases as Dad did. The pro at the club knew he was a fine golfer. So they just signed him up, figuring he'd be proud to accompany his champion son.

When I broke the news one night at dinner, he stomped his foot hard underneath the table and glared at mom. I think he wanted her to help rescue him from yet another social bind, but we both knew she couldn't, not this time.

He didn't say anything to either one of us the rest of supper. Then, when I was lying in bed later that night, he cracked the door to reveal his silhouette. *Jack,* he sighed, *it looks like I've no choice.*

Not a word more of it was breathed until the day of the championship. We ate breakfast together as we would on any other day. Except that instead of disappearing into his study, he got his hat off the rack in the hall, held the door to the garage open for me, tipped his cap to Mom, and said, *Grace, we'll be back for dinner,* like he was Ben Hogan politely acknowledging a gallery, and off we went.

The course where the father-son was contested was a little nine-holer where, if you had any game, you could hit short irons onto practically every green. There wasn't much rough to speak of, but there were plenty of "design oddities" to compensate. On number six, the one with the old barn guarding the green, Dad left his approach short in a bunker that had wood planks laid at forty-five degree angles to buttress the front.

He pondered his escape for what felt like hours, finally stepping into the sand in those polished wingtips of his—he refused to wear spikes—took his putter out, and ramped the ball right up the boards to kick-in distance.

We were playing with three other kids and their dads, and the kids thought it was the coolest recovery shot ever. Dad tipped his cap when one of the other dads applauded his effort, smiling that little coy smile of his. I holed out for a best-shot par while the old man held the pin.

We were leading by three when we came to the eighth, a pushover par five except for a small pond guarding the front of the green. Dad and I both split the fairway with our drives—both of us had exactly 200 yards left to the pin. I pulled a 3-wood and was deep into my pre-shot routine when I heard the old man say, *Son, you sure you want to hit that?*

I ignored him, of course, swinging with everything I could muster. I was 13 then, and 200 yards, 185 of which was pure carry, was an almost unthinkable shot for a half-pint like me. I stood there, mesmerized by this thing of my own making, my eyes darting from it hanging in the air, to the pond, back to ball, pretty as a painting against the sky.

To this day I don't know how it dropped in the water. I was furious. I cussed out loud...the first time I ever swore in front of the old man. *Son of a bitch,* I said.

Dad didn't say anything. He pulled out his 5-iron—we were playing best shot so we hit from the same place—and, as I watched, still fuming, he swung one of his most elegant swings ever. His ball arced into the blue with perfect trajectory and fell out of heaven like an angel…right into the water, in exactly the same spot as mine.

Cursing the golf gods, I slung my clubs over my shoulder and was marching off toward the drop area when I heard the old man say, *Heads up, Junior.* I turned around and there he was, reloading.

I remember pointing out the drop area, figuring he just hadn't seen it. When it became clear he intended to hit another, I ran back to talk some sense into him. He was stubborn, Dad was, and he kept saying, in a voice barely above a whisper, *Jack, I've got a better one in me.*

Ordinarily, I wouldn't have budged, but the other kids and their dads were watching the whole thing from the edge of the fairway, and the groups behind us were stacking up on the tee. So I stepped aside, hands on my hips, and watched the old man hit another in the drink.

Too bad, Robert, one of the dads called out, and the weird thing was the guy meant it. My old man was one of those rare, good golfers that other people still rooted for even if they were having the worst game of their lives.

Dad put his 5-iron back in the bag, and I breathed a sigh of relief.

I think it might be a 4, he muttered. And, as all of us looked on in disbelief, he pulled out a 4-iron, this time with a breeze in his face.

I was desperate to stop what I knew was a bonehead decision. I wanted people to know what a good golfer Dad was, even if he was a little weird. I wanted us to play next year as reigning champs, and the year after, and the year after that. I wanted to win. And all he could say in his defense was, *I've got a better one in me.*

"No, Dad," I said, planting myself directly between him and the flag.

He looked up from his address position, then back down at the ball.

"I said no!"

"Yes, son." His voice was commanding and sad, all at once.

"Dad, I'm not moving."

"Jackie, you'll move or you'll get a hole in your ear."

He backed off, looked at me cockeyed from underneath that broad-brimmed hat of his, then, after further consideration, re-addressed his shot. From where I stood in front of him, it was like looking down the barrel of a gun right into the whites of the eyes of the rifleman. I could actually see his pupils dilating, dialing in on their target, and I could feel his tendons tighten as he pulled the trigger.

I don't know how he missed me. Reflexively, I spun around to watch his shot arc toward the green. I picked it out midair, a wicked cut, dropping out of the sky, right into the water—right on top of his other two.

I believe that's the best one I have in me, he said.

As he passed, I hit him, hard. I don't think anyone saw it, but I could hear Dad gasp, and I could feel his ribs under my knuckles.

I sucker punched my own father. And all he did was keep walking.

I saw him disappear behind the mounds at the back of the green as I picked my par putt out of the hole. I waited while one of the other fathers went into the locker room to look for him, but he never returned.

I ended up having to withdraw us from the tournament with a two-shot lead and one hell of an easy par four to finish. Dad and I could have won in our sleep.

The rest of the day was torture. The other fathers patted me on the back, saying, *I'm sorry, Jack,* not knowing that I'd popped the old man one in the gut. Others just walked by, *tsk-tsking,* unable even to look at the poor kid whose dad had dumped him. I hid in the cart shed for the better part of the afternoon, unable to face a soul.

I was sitting down there, alone, licking my wounds, when I saw his brown Olds pull up, him behind the wheel whistling a tune. Six o'clock sharp, like always.

We must have sat like that for five minutes, him looking straight ahead, the door wide open for me, the trunk popped, before I finally flung my clubs in and slammed the trunk so hard the whole car shook.

I went back to the cart shed. Eventually, he turned the car off. Until dark he sat there. I was nodding off when I heard the Olds roar to life again, saw the taillights come on, saw the old man ease out the drive in the direction of home.

In response, I did the thing that would hurt him most. I walked the two miles home, making it back just before midnight. I let myself in, and slept late the next morning, just to spite him. That night at dinner, Dad announced he would be taking me to Grum's cabin. He said he wanted to begin his winter hiatus early.

At school, papers were due. Tests needed to be taken. None of it mattered, the old man claimed. I would learn more at Grum's cabin in three weeks than I'd learn in a semester behind a desk.

PERCEPTION

Three

Back then it took a full day to fly to the Left Coast, so when we arrived here at Grum's, the old man's relief was palpable. He hung his hat on that very hook over there, put his hands on his hips, and said with more joy than I'd ever heard in his voice, *Hello, you old Building and Loan!* Then he poked his head in his study, and said, "Now about that wall…"

"What wall?" I asked him.

"The stone wall you're going to build for Grum," he said. "Something for you to cut your teeth on. You didn't think you were going to golf the whole time, did you?"

The wall took me weeks. Dad would wake me up at seven. I'd sit with him while he perked his coffee over this very fire, and then he'd walk with me out to the wall, coffee in hand, to see how far I'd come the day before. I tried to put my foot down. But then there was Grum to contend with. He was an old shepherd, South African by birth, and, rumor had it, a fine amateur golfer in his day. His grandfather had immigrated to the coast from Rhodesia to design golf courses back when Pebble Beach was only a glimmer in a realtor's eye.

All Grum did in life, it seemed, was tend his flock of sheep, and he barely did that. What he mostly did was pester me. After Dad's inspection of my work each morning, Dad would walk the quarter of a mile up the trail to Grum's place, and finish his coffee with Grum at the Big House. Fifteen minutes after Dad had walked back down the trail to the cabin to begin his day's studies, Grum would come ambling down with his cane and sit in a

23

wicker chair beside my rock pile.

Mostly the old geezer talked gibberish ... tribes in Africa with funny names, obscure uses for wool. He could recall what seemed like a hundred different kinds of British sailing ships and rare breeds of sheep. And when he wasn't talking nonsense, or dozing off, or calling me "Stonewall Jack," he would tell me how to build my wall.

He'd make a sound like a whale through its blowhole if I placed a rock where he thought it didn't belong, or he'd say something like, *That stone doesn't want to live there, m' boy.* And on the rare occasion when I would place a stone just right, he would heave a huge sigh, as if I'd just relieved him of his earthly burden. *Aw, 'at's a perfect home for it, m' boy,* he'd say, his face breaking into a toady grin.

In all those weeks, we never once left. Whenever Dad and I needed provisions, we'd get them from Grum. Where Grum got his supplies, I've never been certain. Though I discovered one chilly night, following the bumbling Grum on a hunch when he excused himself to fetch firewood, that he did have a woodshed high in the meadow, beneath a grove of eucalyptus, where he kept not just cedarwood but also cans of provisions—fruit mostly— and chocolate harder than a 600-yard par 5.

The sweet-smelling shed doubled as a workshop where the old shepherd once made golf clubs, judging from the dust-covered glue and tape and orphaned clubheads and shafts littering the floor. He had an anvil, a vice, and a selection of mallets wide enough to play a dozen marimbas. And on the backstop of his workbench, where you'd expect a flyspecked pin-up girl, Grum had instead tacked up two dog-eared, creosote-stained playing cards—not a Jack and an Ace, but a *Calamity* and a *Perception*— at least that's what they read.

Calamity couldn't have been better named, for on it appeared a drawing of a tragically unplayable golf ball clamped in the jaws of an alligator. *Perception,* on the other hand, proved much harder to fathom, with its image of a heavily bearded, eye-patched shepherd holding a club instead of a crook. I figured the cards as lighthearted souvenirs from the old man's buried past, and though I stared at them often, I never once asked Grum about them. After all, I wasn't supposed to know he had a toolshed in the first place.

Meantime, my golf improved by leaps and bounds. I was hitting the ball a country mile thanks to the heavy lifting at the rock pile. And my new status as a stone mason was turning me into quite a little sneak, too. Each morning I'd comb the beach for new finds the tide had washed in...bits of coral, shards of glass, once a spoon, and another time an actual golf ball...probably one I myself had mishit from the meadow. Whatever fanciful bits and bobs I could snag before the seagulls I'd mortar into the wall, mostly to see if my half-blind overseer was on the ball, but also to keep myself entertained. Once I cemented in a plastic doll's head that had washed ashore during a storm, and Grum, squinting at it said, *Ah, that pink one enjoys it there, m' boy.*

On our third week at the cabin, I came in one day from working on the ball and chain, and Dad said that Grum had been to town—wonder of wonders—and had something special for us. We climbed up to the Big House before dinner to collect our surprise, and there, sitting on Grum's rolltop desk, was a journal called *The Seeker* opened to an advert for a golf school. It was called the Evalon Island Golf Academy, and it was, Grum said, not far from here. *Why don' y' two give it a whirl,* the old man said. *The wall's all but done. I've a notion to place the last few stones m'self.*

The Academy's last weekend of the season was to commence the following day, and Grum, who was all but blind beyond the eagle eye he directed at my rock wall, said he'd hitch up a team and take us to the ferry, Dad and me being car-less for having flown out to the coast, and Grum being car-less because he preferred to live as they did in the old country.

At the mention of a ferry, I could feel Dad tense up. Even then, he was deathly afraid of deep water. "There's no other way to get there?" he asked.

"'At's right," Grum said. "She's an island, Evalon is."

"I don't think Mom would want us to spend all that money on a golf school," I offered, hoping economics would win out, as it often did in our house.

"Don' worry, Little Robert," Grum said. "Ya more than earned yer keep 'ere, both of ya." Grum sometimes called me *Little Robert,* or *Little Bobby,* because he said I was just like my father. Of course, at the time I thought it fitting that a half-blind man would think that.

The very next morning, Grum pulled up to our cabin in a little cart drawn by two sad-looking nags. By the time we were loaded up, we looked like something from the Irish famine, the three of us and two sets of clubs rumbling down the shoulder of that coastal road while the beautiful cars owned by the beautiful people zoomed by us on those hairpin turns.

When we made it to the ferry port around noon, Grum said, "Looks like I got m' time wrong, m' boys." He hauled himself out of his rickshaw to brush aside some Spanish moss covering an old sign. "Boat to Evalon doesn't leave till well-nigh six," he called out. "But y' boys be fine 'ere till then. Plenty to look at." And with that, Grum shook the reigns and left us, saying he had sheep to tend.

There were a handful of others waiting to take the hours-long boat rides down the coast to the real resorts—the ones I'd heard of. They were newlyweds, and they tickled and teased one another without stop, embarking, Dad and I gathered, on some kind of group honeymoon. They said they'd never heard of Evalon Island. One of the men gave us his card and told us if we liked the links to be sure and let him know.

The old man and I must have waited three hours after the newlyweds bon voyaged. Finally, just before dusk, an old shrimper puttered up, not to the ferry dock where the ticklers had all-aboarded, but to a smaller pier off to the side, in the reeds.

"Boat to Evalon," the ferryman bellowed without looking up. He heaved our bags on the boat like they were baskets full of shrimp. "Well now, that all that's comin'?" he asked once Dad and I were safely aboard. "Name's Charles and this here is yer one-hour, nonstop ferry to Evalon Island. Sit back and enjoy the scenery. And take note of the shepherd's moon. Means bad weather's comin' soon."

By the time we got to the island, the seas had roughened, and I was sick as a dog. Dad was white as a ghost, either out of sea-sickness or from the mere thought of the bottomless depths over which we had passed.

"Easy there, Master Johannes," the ferryman said, helping Dad out onto terra firma. "Them tiger sharks are hungry tonight. Don't want to feed those man-eaters a good soul such as yerself."

"Thank you, Charles. I'm usually more steady on my feet."

"I know, sir. No trouble 't all. And now for the number one son." The boatman reached for me next, heaving me over his shoulder like a sack of potatoes before depositing me on the pier.

"They'll be takin' care of ye inside," he said, backing the boat up slowly into the chop. "Better get the old battleship tied down before all hell breaks loose."

Dad nodded his farewell to the ferryman, picked up his suitcase, put his hat back on, and looked up at the lodge looming before us. "Well, what do you know?" he said. He reached for my hand. "Just what kind of a place do you think Grum has shipped us off to, Jackie?"

From the dock we clambered up a steep flight of stone stairs right through the front door of the Evalon lodge, where a woman who looked as if she'd just woken up from a nap checked us in.

"You must be busy," Dad said. He looked around the cavernous lobby. "A weekend in the fall and all."

"There's a few uns 'round," she said.

"Golfers, you mean?"

"Goffers and the like. There's a few uns 'round."

"Anyone else checking in tonight?"

"No, sir. Weather 'n' all."

Dad raised an eyebrow. "Expecting a bad blow?"

"Hard t' say. Heavy surf t'night an t'morrow, then fog to beat the band."

"Fog?"

"Aye, plenty."

"Well, we're a hardy pair, aren't we, Jackie? If we can survive Grum's cabin, we can surely handle a spot of fog. Where do we find our room, madame?"

"Floor four." She pointed with her pencil up a long spiral staircase. "The side facing the links. You'll be drawing the shutters tight t'night?"

"Batten down the hatches… Of course we will, mam. Good night."

"G'night, you uns."

We climbed all the way up to the top floor, to what turned out to be more a suite than a room. The beams in the ceiling hung so low Dad had to take off his hat. The windows were all of the nautical sort, the round ones, except for one giant pane that looked out on the Evalon links and on the churned-up, wine-dark sea beyond.

"An attic, " Dad observed, more to himself than to me. He surveyed our surroundings before kneeling to start a fire. "Must be right under the mansard roof judging by the size of these beams." He wrapped his hand around one. "Thank the French for figuring out how to fit an extra story in under the eaves. Helped them avoid taxes, since buildings were taxed by how many floors they had beneath the roof. Genius, really." The old man was filled with useless information like that.

Golf memorabilia decorated our room, floor to beam. Old spoons and baffies rested against every table. Black and white photographs of linksters crowded the walls.

Dad examined each in turn. When he was through, he said, "Golf's greatest dark horses… Francis Ouimet, this fellow here,"—he pointed to a goofy-looking kid with Dumbo ears— "was the poor caddie who beat Vardon and Ray in a playoff at the U.S. Open in Brookline in 1913. He was only 20. And Jack Fleck here was a farm boy from Iowa who beat Hogan in the U.S. Open at Olympic in '55. Handsome devil, wasn't he?"

The old man scratched his head and looked down at his feet, like he did back home when he was trying to puzzle out a particularly difficult court case, or how to fix the vacuum cleaner. "These are two of my greatest golfing heroes."

We talked into the wee hours that first, fateful night at Evalon, Dad and I did, spoke of heroes and goats until the fire burned to embers. Then we latched the shutters tight and crawled into our beds in that Dark Horse room, pulling the blankets over us against the chill air and gathering storm.

ON THE ROCKS

Four

We woke the next morning to a sharp rap on the door. Somehow Dad, who always woke with the sun, had badly overslept.

The old man leapt up out of bed in his sleeping clothes and opened the door to a tall young man in a wool waistcoat, flat cap, and plus fours.

"Mistah Robert and Jack. I believe dah two of yah were tah 'ave a gof lesson wid me dis mahnin. Name's Jacobsen…Jake if yud rathah. I'm yer teachah, one ah dem, anyway."

Dad offered our profuse apologies to the youngish pro, calling over his shoulder, "Jack, up 'n' at 'em. We've got some learning to do."

I ran a comb through my hair real quick and brushed my teeth, Dad doing the same, contorting his face behind me in the mirror as he tried to hit the hard-to-reach places. I'd never seen my father brush his teeth before, and it was everything I could do to keep from splitting a gasket, seeing this shy, serious man making faces like he was trying to get a giggle out of a baby.

"He's a Brahmin," Dad whispered to me at the sink. "From Boston, by the sounds of it."

"He's not Scottish?"

"He's as Brahmin as Robert Frost. I wonder what he's doing all the way out here on the Left Coast."

"Let's ask him."

"Brahmins are not a people who respond well to prying, Jackie, or waiting… Be right out," Dad hollered.

"N' problem," the pro yelled back. "Take yer time."

"A Brahmin golf instructor...," the old man muttered to him-self. "Evalon is turning out to have quite a cast of characters."

We emerged from the bathroom to find Jacobsen sitting on the bed, a quizzical look on his face.

"Dah two of yah get yer winks?"

"Haven't slept better in years, have we, Jackie?"

Jake motioned out the window to a mist so bright and thick it felt as if we were underwater. "Ahfraid there'll be no hittin' gof bahs till she lifts...*if* she lifts. It's a wicked pissah."

The advertisement Grum had clipped had promised personal and group instruction, playing lessons on Evalon's classic links—all kinds of things. It had said nothing about fog.

"I'm sure my son here would love to get out on the course...if the weather clears," Dad said.

"Course he would, Mistah Johannes. But none ah us can change dah weathah. Dat's uptah dem?" He pointed the 7-iron in his hand up at our ceiling, looking heavenward. "Best laid plans ah mice 'n' men..."

Jake walked to the door, stooping as he went. He stood six foot four, easy. "Put on yer civvies, fellas, 'n' meet me down in dah front yahd for our first lesson? I got an idear."

"Be down in a minute," Dad said, buttoning up his collared shirt and laying one out for me on the bed. He was a picky dresser and a snappy one, too.

When we got to the "yahd," we found the young pro sitting on a bench beneath a gnarled old cypress, one that looked like it'd lived its whole life fighting the wind. Two chairs had been arranged to face our Beantown Buddha.

"Where are all the other students?" Dad asked. "Overslept, I suppose."

"Won't be any othah students. I requested a private lesson

wid dah two of yah… Don' yah worry 'bout the dough, Mistah Johannes. I asked to teach yah and yer boy 'ere…anothah silvah linin' tah dis nasty weathah. Mos' ah dah othah guests took the boat out days ago."

"That explains it," Dad mumbled.

"Let's staht by havin' yah play some gof."

I pulled my driver and waited for Jake's instruction.

"Leave dah club in the bag fer now, Junyah. We'll be playin' ah different kind ah gof dis mahnin. I want the two of yah tah figure out how tah play togethah without yer sticks."

Dad and I looked at one another like Jake had just asked us to shake our hips like Elvis. Dad was the first to speak.

"You want us to play a game but without either our clubs or our balls?" Jacobsen nodded. "Must we physically strike the ball or can ours be imaginary play, Mr. Jacobsen?"

"Gotta be dah real thing."

"What do you want us to use for a ball…if…if not a ball?" I asked.

"Uptah yah, Junyah," he said. "But while the two of yah are at it, I'm gonna go tah dah tavern and 'ave a fog-liftah."

"A what?" I asked.

"A be-ah."

"A beer," Dad said, translating. "A little early for that, isn't it Mr. Jacobsen?"

"Na' out East, it ain't." He winked at Dad, and walked past us, twirling his 7-iron.

I looked at the old man and he looked at me, and we both started laughing. Here we'd come all this way—risked our lives on Grum's old paddy wagon and nearly lost our lunch on Charles's old shrimper—to attend a golf school in the fog where we weren't allowed to use our clubs.

"First we need a ball," Dad said, chuckling still. "Or something that will pass for one anyway. Any ideas *Junyah?*" he asked, doing his best impression of Jake.

"A rock?"

"Beach rocks are mostly flat in these parts. Besides, I think our Mr. Jacobsen had in mind something nearer at hand."

We decided to split up, each of us trying to solve the problem in our separate peace, picking things up and giving them a good heft, seeing which was right, and which wasn't. I laughed out loud when I saw the old man tug on a little concrete globe at the top of a fancy cornerpost, just to see if he could wiggle it loose. It would have been a boss ball.

About fifteen minutes into our search, it began to rain, slow at first, but steadier as we went, until finally I heard Dad shout *Eureka!* "It was literally right under our feet the whole time, son … the cypress!" he exclaimed. *"Cupressus sempervirens.* I wonder if our beer-loving Mr. Jacobsen had this elegant solution in mind all along."

Dad placed the cypress cone in my hand. It was almost exactly the size and shape of a golf ball.

"My god, it even looks like a featherie!" he exclaimed.

"A featherie?"

"One of the earliest handmade balls—made out of feathers and stitched leather. Look, the little ridges in the cone almost perfectly mirror seams. Ingenious!"

I pocketed our perfect cone for safekeeping. "What do we use for a club?"

"A stick of some sort," Dad mused, surveying the yard again. "Whoever maintains the grounds of Evalon does a pretty tidy job. I don't see a single limb of windfall."

"Except those," I said, pointing to a set of iron pokers beside an outdoor fireplace.

"That's using your noggin, Jackie! But we'll need a clubhead…
Aha! It appears our otherwise tidy groundskeeper left his digging
spoon behind." Dad pointed to a small, rusted trowel rearing its
soiled head in the black dirt beneath the hedgerow. "Give me
your shoestrings, son."

Putting my laces to use, the old man lashed the digging spoon
to the bottom of the poker, set the cypress cone down gentle as
an Easter egg, and handed the "club" to me for its maiden voyage. The weight of the cast-iron stick gave my swing a little more
oomph than usual. When I made contact, the cone zipped off at a
pretty fair clip… 30 yards at least.

Dad pointed to where a rabbit had burrowed in the front
"yahd." "There's our target, son. How 'bout letting your old man
have a go?"

He strode toward the front of the old hotel, way up near the
bar, and gave the cypress cone a mighty blow. I stood by the hole
as the "ball" sailed toward me, level with our eagle's nest, Dark
Horse room atop the old lodge. Dad's shot dropped out of the fog
to within a short chip of the warren.

We played a round of best ball then, each of us taking turns
with the old poker, until we had completed nine holes and carded
a 39—not bad, considering we'd played our par-three course with
an instrument blunt enough to roll logs.

We were reliving our round when old Jake staggered back
into the "yahd" smelling like a brewery.

"Very proud of yah," he said, clapping us on the back a little
too hard. "Watched dah whole ting from dah bah. Dah two of yah
may make good gofahs yet. Too bad it's still a pissah, or we'd take
dis club"—Jake picked the poker up and give it a graceful whip—
"out on dah links."

"What was the point of your little warm-up lesson, Mr. Jacobsen?" Dad asked. "I suppose you present this riddle to all your students?"

"Nah, just tah dah troublemakahs." Jacobsen grinned. "Dah point, Mistah Johannes, is tah get yah tah see dat dah play is dah thing, like ol' Hamlet said."

"Indeed," Dad said.

"If yah don' 'ave yer creativity, yah ain't got nuttin.' Yah certainly don' 'ave yer game. It's all 'bout usin' yer gray mattah."

Jake continued, "I got a little side wagah goin' wid dah bahman. Hey Joe, bring out the be-ah pitch-ahs, yah lugnut."

As the three of us looked on, a burly arm reached through the service window to set a pitcher down on the ledge that doubled as a walk-up counter.

"Wid room fer head, yah jackass!" Jake scolded him. The hand reappeared, pouring a few tablespoons of excess brew onto the grass.

"Dat's mo' like it," Jake said, waggling our improvised "club." "Now gimme dat cypress cone… Yah know Walter Hagen once played tru a bah, lit-rally."

"Double ur nuttin' says if I land it in the pitch-ah, I chug the pitch-ah of be-ah."

I could tell Dad, however much he disapproved, was as gripped by Jake's brash bet as I was. We had to be at least 50 yards away, and the Brahmin was aiming his cone at an opening not much wider than our rabbit hole.

When the Beantown Bomber swung we could see why kept his day job. His move back and through was long and loose, even with a cast-iron poker. The cone cracked off the makeshift clubhead, topped the lodge's third story, and just barely missed the pitcher.

"Yah no-good cheat-ah," Jake called out. "I saw yah move dat cup."

The bar-arm reappeared, this time giving Jake the one-fingered salute.

"It was an admirable attempt, Mr. Jacobsen," Dad consoled our pro.

Jake hung his head, all Sad Sack. "Mah paht of yer teachin' is tru," he moped. "I promised Ava McIntosh I'd take yah ovah aftah yer mahnin lesson wid me."

"Who's Ava McIntosh?" I asked.

"Dah lady pro at Evalon," Jake said, raising an eyebrow.

FOUND

Five

We followed the Brahmin back of the lodge, where the manicured grounds gave way to a trail leading to a driving range of closely mown grass tucked in the forested hills. Jake rapped on the window of the shack that stood beside the hidden practice tee.

"Der all yers, Ava," he said, bowing slightly to the Nordic-looking blonde who opened the door.

"We're enrolled in your weekend golf academy," Dad stammered. "Isn't ... isn't that right, Jackie?" Dad never was very comfortable around women, especially beautiful ones. He always came off sounding like a father.

I mumbled something in response, but Dad's nerves had the better of him, and he kept right on yammering. "We had a very valuable lesson from Mr. Jacobsen just now." He motioned toward Jake, who took that as his cue to amble back down the hill, still cursing his lost bet. "And I guess, young lady, that you're going to show us something special, too."

"I certainly am," she dripped, motioning us to follow. "That's why y'all came to Evalon, isn't it?" We shadowed her all the way up the footpath beyond the practice tee, through the woods, to where we could see the roof of the hulking lodge below us. The air up there smelled of cinnamon and honey.

"That fragrance," Dad said, stopping to tease the scent from a bloom along the path, "what is it?"

"Precisely what I was going to ask y'all."

"You mean this is our lesson?" I had convinced myself I wasn't going to be allowed to swing a real club all weekend.

43

"It is if y'all learn from it, Jackie." The lilt Ava McIntosh said my name with made me want to agree with her, regardless. She must have been from somewhere down South, but not too far... She had only the slightest of accents.

"You want us to tell you what's lending the woods this... intoxicating perfume?" Dad asked.

"What does that have to do with golf?" I demanded.

"That," she said, patting me on the head, "is exactly what we'll talk about when y'all are done. Y'all see that *junipah* over there?" We followed her fine finger to a tree with a knotted up trunk.

"You mean juniper *trees?*" Dad said, gently correcting our lady pro.

"Do I now?"

Father laid his hand on the trunk, or trunks, to illustrate. "Here's where the second grew into the first. You note a different grain in the wood, and a slightly different hue to the leaves." He reached up and pulled one down, submitting it to Ava as evidence.

"How do y' know, Robert, which tree was first? Which grew into which?"

"An analysis of the rings, if properly carried out, would surely reveal..."

"Are y'all proposing that we cut down that beautiful specimen just so we can determine which grew into which?"

"Absolutely not," Dad hastened to add, as if he'd been unwittingly baited into a case for capital murder. "I simply mean that science offers an answer to the conundrum, if we so choose."

"And do we choose?"

"That depends on the object of your lesson, Ms. McIntosh."

"And if science said that junipah is in fact two trees, what then...? Would we see one tree, or two?"

"One tree, because the two have joined," I offered, trying to be of use.

"On the other hand," Dad pointed out, resting his palm on the braided trunk, "technically there would be two trees, each with distinctive traits."

"Interesting," our hostess drawled. "Y'all's lesson this fine morning is to identify the source of that lovely perfume."

Ava McIntosh was right about one thing: the smell of the woods of Evalon intoxicated. So, bidding our pro a temporary adieu, we walked together, Dad and I, farther up the path through the woods until the fragrance overcame us. Time and again we'd stop, herky-jerky, like a summer night when you're trying to track the one ventriloquist cricket that won't let you sleep.

The old man would rub a leaf between his fingers and breathe deeply, trying to tease out its scent. Then just when we'd think we had the fragrance traced to a particular clump or bloom, we'd put our noses hard to the task again, and we would lose the bouquet—like saying a word over and over until it loses its meaning.

What began as an easy chore turned into an epic frustration, worse than golf itself. Even Dad appeared ready to tear out what remained of his hair, kneeling before plant after plant, working his olfactory like an Irish setter on sensory overload.

For a while he suspected a coastal shrub called coyote brush. Next I called him over to sniff some mint. Shortly thereafter we came upon a clump of wild anise, which had a licorice scent… cinnamon if you used your imagination. And then, too, there was honeysuckle, and sage, and even pine and cypress, which Dad said the Egyptians perfumed their coffins with.

By the time we stopped, the sun had moved directly overhead, the rays finally figuring a way down to the forest floor. Dad mopped the sweat from his forehead with a handkerchief. "Son, I don't know up from down anymore. Ms. McIntosh has set us an admirable test, much harder, in its way, than Mr. Jacobsen's." In my one-track mind, I was worried that if we failed, we wouldn't get to golf.

Defeated, we wandered down the trail back to the practice tee, Dad stopping to stir the scent from one or two final blossoms, shaking his head. It was the first time I ever saw him completely stumped.

Ava stood when we entered her shed, straightening her skirt. "Y'all have an answer?"

Dad spoke first. "Jack and I accepted your challenge in good faith, Ms. McIntosh, but we cannot say, with anything approaching certainty, which plant produces that exquisite scent."

Our teacher looked momentarily crestfallen. "What can you tell me, boys?"

"Jackie identified mint, pine, and sage, the latter of which he knows well from his mother's kitchen."

Ava nodded. "And you, Robert?"

"I detected cypress, eucalyptus, and something I suspect comes from that curious species *Baccharis,* coyote brush."

"I asked y'all to determine the source of that inimitable perfume, and y'all give me seven answers, none more correct than the other?"

"I'm afraid so." Dad hung his head. I watched our teacher's face intently, awaiting her reaction.

"It's a perfectly reasonable answer," she said at last. "Fair, disciplined, honest. Though something less than definitive, y'all understand?"

We nodded.

She extended her hand, first to Dad, then to me. "Congratulations. Y'all have passed your first examination."

"But we didn't get it right," I protested.

"On the contrary, Jackie. Y'all couldn't be more correct. The question has many answers ... to suggest one at the expense of the other is the only way y'all could err. That's why I chose the woodland bouquet ... It's all the scents all y'all mentioned, and more. Its intoxication is in its combination."

Dad chuckled, out of relief or nervousness, it was hard to say. "Another valuable lesson for an old man as well as a young one."

"What does it have to do with golf?" I demanded. I had half a mind to tell Ms. Dixie that we hadn't come to a golf academy to study field botany, but Dad wisely shushed me.

"Howsabout answering your own question, Young Jack," she said. "What *does* it have to do with gof?" I loved the molasses drip way she said *gof*, too ... just like the unflappable, well-tanned pros on TV. "Tell me, have you ever had a mechanical breakdown in your gof swing?"

"Sure," I said, "lots of times."

"Have you ever had more than one 'breakdown' at once?"

I nodded again.

"How then do y'all fix a problem that isn't a single problem at all, but the contribution of many parts? Like that junipah tree we were talkin' about just now, the one with two trunks... A golf swing isn't all wrong or all right is it, Jackie? If it were all wrong, surely y'all wouldn't be able to even hit a gof ball. And if it were all one-hundred-percent right, every cotton-pickin' part would be flawless on every pass. Every swing, gentlemen, is a combination of movements well-timed and out-of-time. A swing is the sum of its imperfections."

"Like the swinger of the club," Dad said, grinning. "The man behind the machine, as it were."

"Or the lady... In any case, imperfection is perfection. Purity in golf or in life paves a path to perdition."

Dad must have seen me furrow my brow, because he said, "What Ava means, Jack, is 'that dog won't hunt.' The perfectionist barks up the wrong tree."

She nodded in agreement, suggesting the matter closed. "I suppose y'all would like to see your pro hit a gof ball before you go, 'specially since she's a lady. She's got to prove herself, doesn't she?"

Ava grabbed a 9-iron that had been leaning against the door jamb, and headed outside. She glanced over her shoulder coyly, as if to say, *Comin', boys?*

On the practice tee the only thing I could make out in the fog was our teacher's bright red baseball cap and her ponytail of sandy blonde. Dad stopped at the edge of the tee, a bemused look on his face.

Ms. Dixie made a couple easy passes, holding beautiful positions both at the top and at the finish. After she'd made a dozen or so rehearsals, she rolled a ball into position with her clubhead, shuffled her feet into alignment, and swung with a force and grace I'd never seen from a woman. The ball rocketed into the mist.

She performed this feat several times over, each time with absolute concentration, then stopped, cocking her head at me, that ponytail of hers swinging behind her. "What do y'all think?"

"They sound great," I admitted. "Except I can't see them. The fog's too thick."

"Is it necessary to see them, Jackie? What if I told y'all the last three have been perfect?"

I glanced over at Dad, who appeared to be enjoying our discourse.

"I'd believe you," I said.

"Why would you believe me?"

"Because they're your shots."

"And why am I better qualified than y'all to decide whether they're good shots?"

"Because...you made them."

"Does that fact make me a more reliable witness? The cook can't taste her own soup." Ava laughed beautifully. "Let's return to y'all's original premise. Do you have to see your shots to know whether they're good?"

"You do if you want to know how close to the target they finish."

She struck another shot into the bright white blanket of sky, purring, "I promise y'all that one was nothin' short of divine."

"A gof shot begins as a dream," our lady pro continued, "or a nightmare. Either way, it's a vision. When the swing begins, the dream doesn't end, does it?"

At that point, the old man stepped forward, uncrossing his arms and shoving them in his pockets. "What if I argue the opposite, Ms. McIntosh, that the dream ends when the swing begins. That is when the dream necessarily takes shape and form, and becomes real, which, inevitably means its results are judged good or bad."

"A fair point, Robert," she said, pausing to hit another bullet into the fog's wet blanket. "But by your argument, the shot I just struck wasn't real, because it did not assume a form or a shape either of us could witness. Yet, by the gods of golf, I swear my shot was as real as the nose on my face."

"And a pretty nose it is, Ms. McIntosh." It was the first time I ever heard the old man say anything the least bit flirty to a woman. He must have been smitten with our Ms. Dixie, and who could blame him?

Ava handed me her 9-iron, stepped back beside Dad, and said,

"Why don't you give it whirl?"

The fog seemed to thicken as I addressed one of our teacher's bright white pills, thickened so much that the ball itself seemed to dematerialize. I rushed my motion, closing the clubface down as I made contact, hitting it off the toe, I'm sure, though the ball left no mark.

"How was it, Young Jack?" she asked.

"God-awful," I groaned, almost slamming the club down before I remembered it wasn't mine to slam. "Probably no more than 80 yards."

"Probably?"

I waved Ava's short iron around in the murk. "There's no way of knowing... between all your identical practice balls laying out on the range and this fog."

"Is it not just as possible that your 'god-awful' stroke finished exactly on target... that your perception of your swing is flawed, not the swing itself?"

"I guess," I confessed.

"And what if the shot itself was not poor, but the dream of the shot that set it in motion. What then?"

"Then I'd have to dream a better dream."

She rolled another perfectly white pearl in front of me and said, "Why not do it then?"

I set up to it, waggling, looking down my target line into a bright white nothing.

"The fog is nothing but a screen for your own imaginings, like a bed sheet strung between two trees on which you're projecting your own movie. Make it a good movie, Jackie."

I'm not sure if I hit that shot off the toe or not—I think maybe so—but when I looked into the dew to follow its flight, I envisioned it heading straight and true.

"Well-struck, Jackie!" Dad cheered, though I knew he couldn't have seen the shot either. Maybe he'd had the same dream I'd had.

We talked a bit more on the range after that, the three of us ghosts to one another, so dense had the fog become. But in a strange way we were more real to one another than we had been an hour ago. Dad himself had become more familiar somehow, very unlike the shadow I knew back home, or at Grum's. His features seemed to soften in the Evalon haze. Even his hat, which could seem rakish, appeared rounded.

Years later, when I was a cocky art major in college, my drawing professor would put a bowl of apples and oranges out for us disciples to practice on. Almost to spite him, I'd paint his ho-hum still-life spot on—perfect likenesses every time—until one day he stopped at my drawing table to tell me my work revealed nothing. He demanded that I squint at the scene before me in order to truly see it. When I did, I thought about Dad, about that precise moment on the practice tee in the woods at Evalon, and about Ava McIntosh, pretty as a vision. My painting prof claimed that in the blur of a squint existed an object's—or a person's—truer shape.

That's how Dad appeared to me that first afternoon at Evalon. And I wonder now if I seemed any different to him. He seemed to like me better as we stood there chatting, seemed happier in my presence, seemed to regard me from that point forward as an equal.

After a while, a member of the lodge staff, a bellboy, came to fetch us, breaking the spell Ms. McIntosh had cast. He informed us that Mr. Jacobsen was, as he put it, "indisposed of," and that we had been scheduled for an afternoon session in the library. The bellhop, sensing my disappointment, gestured at the fog as if to say, *It's out of my hands, fellas.*

As soon as the bellboy deposited us at the hotel, I reverted to my old self—the spoiled, demanding brat whose father could do no right. I let the old man have it. "We're being sent to study hall because our pro is a drunk. This is some golf academy, Dad. Do something."

But asking the old man to risk confrontation was fruitless, and I knew it. I might as well have asked him do an Irish jig. It wasn't in his nature. Besides, as he pointed out, Evalon had its own way of teaching.

SLICE

Six

In the afternoon, we wandered downstairs to the library and let ourselves in. We had been advised to find the archivist—one Augustus Repartee—who would be in charge of our "instruction."

We found him at his desk in an alcove off the main reading room. He sported ginger hair and wore a mustache and a wrinkled, olive green golf shirt two sizes too small. He was smoking when we opened the door, saddle shoes up on his desk.

For the first time since our arrival, we saw other guests— a foursome of them—seated around one of the library tables playing what looked to be an intense game of cards. They barely looked up as we followed Augustus to the rooms where our tour would begin.

"Don't mind them," he said with barely disguised disdain. "They really shouldn't be here, unless you consider that confounded game research."

"What are they playing?" I asked.

"It's called *Soule,* and it's an utter waste of time," he sniffed. The more Augustus talked with his stiff upper lip the more English he sounded to me, though he later claimed to be from New Jersey. Dad said his strange way of speaking probably had as much to do with his profession as his geography. "You'll be learning about Soule soon enough. Everyone who comes to Evalon must, at some juncture."

"Quite a collection you've assembled here, Mr. Repartee," Dad said, craning his neck to examine the books on the highest shelves. "You must have tens of thousands of volumes."

"Not including our special collections," Augustus said, pleased at the attention. "Clearly you're an appreciator of fine libraries."

"I have a respectable one of my own at home," Dad said, and he did, though I hadn't had occasion to see it very often. The old man was as private about his books as he was about his life.

"As you might imagine, we here at Evalon specialize in volumes penned by the greatest players ever to lace up a pair of spikes. This, for example," Augustus said, whipping a leather-bound volume off the shelf, "is an autographed first edition of Bobby Jones's *Down the Fairway*. Would you like to handle it?"

"I shouldn't, Mr. Repartee," I said.

"Nonsense, Young Jack, and please, my friends call me Augustus, or Auggie. Evalon is meant to be a hands-on experience."

"Go ahead, Jackie," Dad urged, so I cracked the book to gawk at Bobby Jones's youthful signature, before passing it on, like a newborn, to the old man.

"Never thought I'd see the day... a Bobby Jones original," he whistled.

"That's just the beginning," Augustus said, as Dad passed the volume back to him gingerly. "You two look like the kind who might be interested in our archival collections."

We followed the archivist down a short hall, stopping at the first door on our left. Augustus fumbled with his keys, trying several before he found the winner. "Don't often bring guests in here," he muttered.

The room we entered wasn't much bigger than Grum's cabin, and there wasn't a single window in it. In the corner, a small machine hummed, keeping the air at just the right humidity.

"This," Augustus said solemnly, "is the world's only collection of divots." He pulled a file folder marked "P" down from a shelf near at hand. "This, for example," he said, fetching from the file what looked like a large baggie of loose tea, "is Gary Player's divot from the 1955 Egyptian Matchplay. It's sandier than most."

"All of these are actual divots from the greatest golfers of all time?" I asked, incredulous.

Dad put his hand on top of my head. "Mr. Repartee is clearly pulling our leg, son. No one saves divots."

Augustus cocked his head. "Is that so, Mr. Johannes? Have you ever lingered at a tournament looking for souvenirs after the sun has gone down and the fans have gone home? Have you ever hired a hungry caddie in the days before today's hefty tournament payouts. Take it from me and the network of Evalon alumni invested in our collection, a starving caddie can be convinced to perform most any service. Money talks." He grinned. "Most people consider the divot a relatively incidental part of the game. But it is actually a golfer's signature, his trademark carved in the soil of the stadium wherein he creates his most enduring legacy."

"A Jack Nicklaus divot," the librarian continued, "is completely different than a Chi-Chi Rodriguez divot, which is prone to disintegration. In any case, preserving the divot is the equivalent of creating a death mask…a plaster mold…of a great man at the exact moment when his spirit passes from this mortal life. It's a timeless impression, every bit as unique as a fingerprint."

"Our latest initiative involves collecting the first divots of juniors destined for golfing fame. In fact, we've just acquired an early Nicklaus from the range at Scioto County Club in Columbus, Ohio, from the very practice tee where the Golden Bear first took instruction from Jack Grout."

"Think of the provenance on that one," Dad whistled, clearly convinced now by Augustus's pitch.

"Provenance indeed…the history of ownership, the special significance or certifiable origin of an antique…exactly, Mr.

Johannes. In the future it may be possible to grow from these for-gotten remnants exact replicas. Imagine being able to cultivate in your front lawn the very rye that grew beneath Bobby Jones's feet the inaugural year of the Masters."

"You all right in there, Auggie?" one of the card players called out halfheartedly from the main room.

"Just fine," the archivist called back, then, under his breath, "just keep on with that life-wasting pursuit of yours…" Auggie cleared his throat. "In any case, I am convinced this collection will one day be one of the most valuable in all of golf, if it isn't already... Shall we, gentlemen?"

Dad and I filed out of the divot room, still in awe, as Auggie continued with his tour. "Our next stop, the Legacy Room, is as important as the divot collection in my estimation. And as before, ours is the only archive of its kind in the world."

The archivist opened the door to a cramped room similar to the last, only brighter, and filled with books rather than airtight plastic bags.

"The Legacy Room, as its name indicates, preserves the parting thoughts of select golfers bestowed the honor of playing Evalon's unrivaled links."

"The volumes in this room record the dying philosophies of every golfer ever to play Evalon?" Dad asked, open-mouthed at the morbid wonder of it.

"Anyone at or over the ripe old age of sixty, and within six months of his or her untimely passing."

"I just turned sixty," Dad offered.

We'd thrown a small party for him up at the Big House, com-plete with an angel food cake Grum picked up in town, and a cel-ebratory shot into the ocean for each of us with Grum's favorite 5-iron—the one Dad claimed the old goat brought out only for the most special occasions.

"How can one know when one's time is coming?" Dad asked, still pondering.

"Most accomplished linksters," Augustus explained, "have a keen sixth sense for coming events. That's why they're so much better than the average human at visualization, allowing them to predict, for instance, the next, unseen breeze."

"How do you determine who should write their legacy?"

"Actuarial science long ago revealed a curious spike in morbidity among golfers reaching the landmark age of 60. When our age-appropriate golfers leave Evalon, we simply cross check our guest list against the following year's public death records."

"And whose grisly job is that?" Dad asked.

"Mine," Augustus said, bowing. "Actually, it's quite satisfying to be the scribe of such irreplaceable wisdoms. We give our golfers the amount of space they would be given on a tombstone to communicate something vital learned about the game, or about life. Often our golfers are surprised to learn their epitaphs apply equally to both. Thus these volumes," the archivist continued, "all contain a short adage. Please, browse at your leisure."

"Go on, Junior," Dad said, giving me a nudge.

I pulled a random volume off the shelf and read aloud:

Don't cut doglegs unless you're prepared to be bitten.

Another said:

She was clearly out of bounds.

Another read:

Clarice, I was wrong.

Still another wrote:

Choose your partners wisely. They witness both your aces and your empty hands.

And finally:

Birds that sing at twilight have the prettiest songs.

"*Birds* or *birdies,* do you suppose?" Augustus punned.

"If the whole idea is to leave a message behind that people will learn from, why are these so mysterious?" I asked.

"Because, son, when you're limited to what you can fit on a tombstone, you inevitably turn to poetry," Dad explained. "And poetry is poetry because it's a blend of what must go unsaid and what must be said. Jackie, just for the hell of it, let's see if there are any Johannes that have been to Evalon."

The gesture surprised me, but then the old man and I always looked up our last name in the phonebook when we traveled, just because.

I moved my finger down the list of "Js" to an entry for Caspar Johannes, date of death 1948, cause of death, unknown, birthplace, Brussels, Holland, place of residence at time of death, Evalon Island.

"Let me see that," Dad demanded after I read the entry aloud. I handed the book to him. "Jackie," he said, wide-eyed, "this is your grandfather, my dad, the one I never knew. He was here ... at Evalon."

Someone had to end it.

The old man read Caspar Johannes's legacy out loud yet again, letting it sink in. "It's the only thing I've ever read written in his own hand, outside of the letters he wrote Mom when he was overseas. Augustus, this is an absolute treasure. May I take it home to share with my wife?"

"I'm afraid I cannot allow that, Robert, much as I would like. The legacy papers are what we call in the trade a 'restricted item.' They must remain here for the enlightenment of all golfers who visit us."

"In any case, gents," our tour guide said, turning brisk again, "it is well-nigh five o'clock. However, you will be glad to know that due to the abbreviated nature of your tour, I have arranged for your after-hours access to our final archive: The Witness Room... a collection devoted to the documented mystical or religious experiences of golfers here at Evalon. It is a controversial collection, as there is much debate over the veracity of the field notes and sketches contained therein."

"The collection is limited to documented phenomena observed here on the Island. I have also made the decision, politically unpopular as it may be, to include relevant narratives of the patients who received treatment here during and after the war, when our lodge served as a veteran's hospital and, later, a private mental institution. Our famous links were designed as a theater... a laboratory, really... for a new kind of therapy, enlightenment and serenity achieved through golf."

Augustus painstakingly replaced the volumes he'd pulled from the shelf as Dad and I mulled over his revelation. "There are perhaps a dozen boxes of ephemera. There would be many, many, more, but, regrettably, many of the clinical notes were burned by those who found such observational therapy to invite negative press."

Augustus removed a skeleton key from the giant ring clipped to his belt loop and placed it in Dad's hand. Together, the three of us wandered back to the reading room, our librarian-guide rousing the card players from their apparent stupor, shooing them out the door to much grumbling and taunts of *spoilsport.*

"Have a wonderful night here in Evalon," Augustus said to Dad and me as he bade us farewell at the door. "Your key to the Witness Room also opens the main library. They are yours for an evening, gentlemen, the keys to the proverbial castle."

SWEET SPOT

Seven

Dad and I ate in a rush that night, seeing no one beyond the skeleton Evalon staff and the few old geezers who had been playing Soule in the library earlier that afternoon.

The Great Hall at Evalon, where the meals were served, sprawled, and the old gents seemed lost in it. When the foursome of geriatric card sharks passed Dad and me, they mumbled something like *Good evening, gentlemen,* but they didn't stop to chat. Their speech sounded mechanical, disinterested, as if we could pull their strings and from them would issue one of a half dozen vaguely appropriate greetings.

The food itself, as we might have expected on an island with such sporadic contact with the mainland, was strictly out-of-the-can. In the corner of the cafeteria, an old woman pianist with long white fingers played plucky show tunes in a voice that would crack glass. Dad and I cringed every time she belted out a number or when, between songs, the old dame flirted shamelessly with the geezers.

We spotted Jacobsen on his way out of the Evalon lounge, "be-ah" in hand. Probably, Dad and I figured, the pros could eat for free as part of their compensation. Where else on the Island would they find any grub? Jake stopped briefly at our table to ask how our lesson with Ava had gone. He informed us that tomorrow morning, rain or shine, our lessons would continue.

After dinner, we wandered down the deserted hall to the library and unlocked the door, whispering like a couple of prowlers in the echo-chamber of the lodge. We didn't know if Auggie had cleared our after-hours entry with his bosses, or whether our access had been his own call. We figured him for the type to make his own executive decisions. After all, it had been through his efforts that the special collections had been initiated in the first place.

We unlocked the door to the reading room, turning on as few lights as possible, and made a beeline for the archives. Compared to the other rooms, which were carpeted and bright, the Witness Room felt mortuary. Dust clung to the wood floors and to the surfaces of drawers recessed in the walls like burial vaults. I held the flashlight while Dad read aloud the aluminum labels mounted on each of the drawers.

Demons. The old man read the tag aloud, using his index finger to trace the print left to right in the semi-darkness. Wordless, he hefted the drawer down, wrestling it onto the room's only table. Inside, countless hanging file folders, many of them stamped with the label Evalon Institute for the Mentally Insane, rattled on rails. Dad pulled a folder out at random and opened it in his lap while I held the light over his shoulder.

Before us lay picture after picture of just what the label had promised: demons. Some were shown hovering over hapless dinners in a cafeteria; some were shown peering out from behind kitchen hutches while a family talked, unawares. Some showed demons hovering over a man lying in bedclothes, presumably asleep. Most captured the demons outside, on a golf course, it appeared, emerging jinni-like from the hole in a swirl of flame or brimstone, or hurling fire or sulfur from twisted tree branches.

"The collection note says the patients played golf as a treatment for shellshock and other war injuries. Look at these drawings, Jackie. They're fantastic, and tortured."

Page after page traced imps of every size and shape. All

seemed in the midst of dirty deeds, deeds conjured by the very act of playing golf. To some was stapled a typed note with letterhead reading, *Dr. Harlan Cragg, Chief Psychologist.* On each, Dr. Cragg had recorded the time and setting in which the drawing had been made. In some he had appended editorial notes such as *possibly delusional* or *likely schizoid.* In others the doctor had jotted comments such as *possible phantasm.*

As the dates moved closer to the present, the files grew fewer. 1950 was the last file we saw bearing the stamp of the Evalon Institute for the Mentally Insane and the last to record Dr. Harlan Cragg as supervising psychologist. The final entry, dated some ten years before our visit, portrayed what looked like two giant cat's eyes peering out from a layer of fog hovering over the ocean. The back of the sketch read *as seen on the 8th hole.*

Soule—Clinical Observations—Recorded Weather Conditions—Aromatic and Psychotropic Plants. Dad's index finger hovered over the label marked *Soule.* Again, he brought the heavy oak drawer down with a grunt, and again I held the light while he spread the contents of the folder on his lap for inspection.

Apparently, Soule—the game that Augustus had hassled the geezers for playing earlier that afternoon—enjoyed a long history at Evalon. Notes within the folder suggested a Dutch origin for the game of chance, while others implied that it had been invented by the mental patients themselves during long periods of convalescence on the Island.

The file contained photographs of what looked to Dad and me like an early, black and white version of the Great Hall we had dined in just an hour before, showing table after table of patients in matching scrubs holding cards in their hands, four players to every table. In one photo, it appeared as if there were a hundred tables full of contestants. The caption on the back read, *Soule*

Shotgun Start, 1946.

The rest of the folder archived what we guessed were Soule scorecards, each one showing a complicated gridwork of miniature icons that looked almost like Egyptian hieroglyphics, accompanied by a series of numerical scores on each of 18 holes—either three, four, or five, as in golf.

We found no mention of the rules of the game, nor any official recording of the winners of the tournament. The file ended with a cartoon captioned *The Soule King* that showed a balding, beamish man with an unruly sprig of hair combed over a shiny scalp. The illustration captured him marching up to the podium to receive a trophy from a man in doctor's garb. The cartoonist had drawn a halo over the lucky winner's head, placing him in stark contrast to the room full of sufferers beyond, who were depicted in various stages of self-mutilation... some with clumps of hair pulled out, others with blood-shot eyes, still others fending off hounds nipping at the loose ends of their scrubs.

I wanted to scream there in that dark, claustrophobic room, but Dad held his finger to his lips and pointed to a drawer directly in front of us, smack-dab in the middle of the vaulted cabinet. It read *Golf Gods.*

He pulled the drawer down eagerly—too eagerly. He stopped its free fall with his knee, wincing as the drawer crashed down on the tabletop. We listened closely, wondering if the racket might have alerted the lodge staff to our presence.

The drawer turned out exactly as advertised, sketches—field notes, really—of what appeared to be golfing deities. Some of the drawings were stamped with the mental institute's logotype, others not.

Dad pointed a trembling finger at a scrawl in the lower right-hand corner of the first couple of drawings, gestural sketches showing figures fleeting as fairies. "I'd know that John Hancock anywhere. That, Jackie, is the unmistakable hand of your grandfather." He raised his hand to quiet me. "These are *his* drawings." Dad rifled through the remaining sketches as if he believed they'd disappear in his hands.

He fanned a half dozen of the pictures out on the table. The first one read *Draw and Claw* and showed a strong-jawed, clean-shaven man, rendered quickly, contemplating his putt on the eighth hole with a bulldog beside him. The date read 8/19/44. Another, drawn three days later, showed the same figure—presumably Draw—in the follow through of a classic swing. He wore a wool flat cap, a checkered sweater vest, and knickers.

Dad pointed next to a sketch dated almost exactly one year later, 8/17/45. Grandpa had drawn a woman this time with bobbed hair wearing a sun hat and skirt. A second sketch on the very same page showed her startled, pretty face, lips parted as if she herself had seen a ghost. The caption read: *Fade noticed me. Faded away.*

Poor Caspar must have ground his pencil to a nub laying in the heavy lines of the next drawing, which bore the tagline: *Hook and her minion harassing a caddie.* The looper was shown at full gallop, a pinscher nipping at his trousers. A second drawing showed the much-feared goddess slouched low and scheming in a high-backed chair, fingers interlocked in front of pouty lips.

I pointed out to Dad that the framed painting on the wall behind Hook in Caspar's drawing—showing a rugged chain of mountains with the sea beyond—was exactly the picture that hung at the corner of the hall leading to Evalon's library—the very hall through which we had passed minutes before.

"I noticed the same thing," he said, almost wearily, as if a great weight had just landed on him.

The final photo in what Augustus or some other archivist had classified as "gesturals" pictured a beautiful young blonde, hair bobbed. She wore a handsome cloche, her right arm shading her eyes as she peered into the heavens. *Checking the height of the ball,* the caption read. Beside her a Canadian goose crooked its long neck skyward.

For the longest time, Dad said nothing. He replaced the sketches in their folder, handling them as if they were the Declaration of Independence, before pulling out another folder, this one labeled *Finished Studies.*

These proved more elaborate still, the works of weeks if not months, and on these too was stamped *Evalon Institute for the Mentally Insane.* The drawings portrayed the same cast of characters, but they were details, as if in the interim Caspar had somehow become well-acquainted with his subjects, and they with him. The first pictured the handsome, open-faced young man in a flat cap along with his bulldog. In back of them loomed an imposing building—unmistakably the Evalon Lodge—and an orchard.

The rest of the figure studies followed suit: in one image the goddess Caspar had earlier labeled Fade tipped her cap coquettishly. In another, Hook, wearing her pearls and pillbox again, darkened the bar at the lodge, drawing angry looks.

The final study documented a new character, a big, handsome devil with hard eyes and raven hair. Beneath a broad-brimmed, banded hat, his eyebrow arched menacingly. Behind him a golf inferno raged.

"Slice," Dad said.

"How do you know?"

"Call it a son's intuition." Then, after a pause. "We have Fade and Draw. We have Hook. What's the antithesis of a hook, and the amateur golfer's greatest nemesis ... ?"

"Slice."

"You got it, Junior."

"Why are these drawings stamped with the mental institute's name and not the hospital's?" I asked.

"Two possible reasons, so far as I can figure," Dad said. "First explanation—something clerical—maybe a change in director or archivist. Or"—another pause, this one more dramatic—"maybe Caspar wasn't just here when the military ran the hospital…"

"You mean…?"

"It's possible, Jackie. Maybe Caspar wasn't…playing with a full deck."

"Maybe he worked at Evalon."

"Maybe, but I suspect if he was in the employ of the Institute these drawings would list his official title. If you look closely, you'll notice there's a number on his studies. Almost certainly Dad's patient number, 9. And Jack…"

"Ya, Dad?"

"These drawings are of golf gods…mythical beings…invisible…at least to most. Sketches like these would be exactly the kind of thing that would get you transferred from a veteran's hospital to a psych ward, or cause you to 'stay over' when the place changed hands from public to private, and began specializing in psychological disorders."

"I've heard you talk about the gods of golf before." Dad looked startled when I said it, as if a dark secret had come to light.

"You have?"

"All those tournaments you picked me up from. On the way home…when I'd describe a really good shot, or a really bad one… you'd say, *The gods of golf can be fickle, Jackie.*"

The old man looked as if he had just been confronted with irrefutable evidence. "So I did."

"Do you believe in them?" I walked around front of the table, accidentally shining the light right in his eyes.

Dad folded and unfolded his hands several times before he answered. "How could I not?" he said at last. "Golf is a consummate game of skill, but it is also a consummate game of chance. And when chance and uncertainly exist to a great degree in any of man's endeavors"—I knew he was nervous because he always used big words when he was nervous—"there exists a corresponding level of faith, and where there is faith, son, there is divinity."

"For the record,"—I repeated the question, giving the old man a taste of his own lawyerly medicine—"do the gods of golf exist?"

"Yes, Your Honor."

I felt sorry for him in the silence that followed his admission, having to find out that his father, a father he never had the chance to meet, was not only wounded in war, but was also, more than likely, a loon. And I felt guilty, too, that I had grilled the old man about his beliefs. At that moment, sitting there under the white light, Dad seemed small and old, stripped down almost.

Just then we heard a racket coming from the reading room. Dad held his finger to his lips, quickly setting the archive back exactly as we had found it. He moved to the door, motioning me to follow.

We tiptoed down the hall that housed Auggie's archives—past the Legacy Room, past the divot collection, and into the antechamber leading to the reading room, where Dad stopped to put his ear to the door, mouthing the word *voices*. He opened it slowly, just enough for us to peek through.

Gathered around the table were the same four geezers we'd seen in the library earlier that afternoon and at dinner. They had turned the table lamp on but kept the overhead lights off, shadowing their faces. They whispered as if they were covering a golf match, busying themselves about their usual trick: dealing cards.

Every so often, one of the old fogies would say *play away*. At intervals they'd express approval or disapproval—*rough luck* or *bold stroke,* they'd say. But mostly theirs appeared to be a game played in silence, a game the foursome had played so many times they could almost play it in their sleep. From afar, the only action appeared to be the frequent drawing and displaying of cards.

Three times in the minutes Dad and I watched from our hiding place, one or another of the players stopped to consult a tome that rested on the side of the table. The book was bigger than the biggest dictionary I'd ever seen. The sound of its opening and closing made a heavy thump—no doubt the noise that had startled us back in the Witness Room.

The old man and I were trapped. The only way out of the library was past the card game, which appeared to be going on in secret. While I stood there, weighing our options, Dad reached through the crack in the door, flipped on the overhead light, and strode through the portal, hoping, I guess, that I'd follow suit.

"Evening, gentlemen," he said. They blinked, pale and mole-like. "I'm afraid the reading room is closed." Dad waved the skeleton key Augustus had given us.

The geezers, initially startled, resumed their game, unperturbed. "We'll play through if you don't mind," one of the gents droned, tipping his visor.

"Nobody here but us chickens," another said.

"Augustus charged me with closing the library," Dad repeated. "I'm sure you realize it's after-hours."

"Dear Augustus," one of them mused, "I'm sure he wouldn't mind if four old men played a harmless match."

Dad hadn't counted on his bluff meeting such resistance.

"How much longer do you think you'll be?" he asked finally. "Jack and I could finish some work in the archives if you'll wrap up."

The big, fleshly fellow sitting center-table—the grand poobah, apparently—laughed heartily. "We won't be finishing this game for a *very, very* long time." He looked at each of his three playing companions before correcting himself. "Rather, I should say it is *a possibility* that we might complete our round, but the likelihood of that happening today, or next week, or next month, young man, is infinitely unlikely."

"Might as well wait for a bolt of lightening," another chimed.

While Dad suffered their blathering, I tried to sneak a peek at their cards, but each dude was playing them, as the old saying goes, close to the vest.

"I suppose what I could do," Dad said, hoping, no doubt, to light a fire under them. "Is simply advise Augustus that the four of you are continuing your game after closing time."

"As you wish," one said. He yawned as he drew another card. However it was played, the game must have been engrossing. Each of the foursome seemed lost in concentration.

"Jackie and I will leave you gentlemen to your cards and go notify Augustus then." Dad nodded to me and held out his hand. I took it, and we walked together out the front door of the library, shutting the light off, and locking up behind us.

Once we'd closed the door on the Soule match, the old man fished in his pocket for the business card Augustus had given him earlier that afternoon. "We'll have the front desk ring him," he said, marching me downstairs to the lobby. "He must live somewhere here on the Island."

The night clerk, the same spooky gray-hair that had checked us in the first night, appeared happy to have someone to assist. She had Augustus on the line with a few quick twists of a rotary phone. "Which 'uns is calling?" she asked, putting her hand over the receiver.

"Tell him it's Robert and Jack," Dad said. "Tell him it's important."

TAX AUDIT

Eight

Augustus waited for us at the door to Room 72 dressed in a plaid, tasseled smoking jacket and slippers. His hair was mussed.

"What brings you to me at this late hour," the archivist asked, lighting up a pipe as he invited us in.

"We visited the Witness Room…"

"I hoped you might."

"…and found there some very remarkable things." Dad paused, glancing over at me. "But that's not what we came to talk about. At least, not why we came at this hour."

"Oh?" Augustus raised a caterpillar eyebrow.

"We wanted to alert you that the card players…the four old gentlemen you shooed away this afternoon…are at it again."

The archivist stomped his slippered foot on the floor. "How in the world did they…."

"I'm afraid I neglected to lock the door behind us when we entered," Dad said, eyes downcast.

"Always waiting their chance to play that infernal game." Augustus shook his head vigorously. "Officially, it's forbidden on Evalon Island by order of Harlan Cragg himself. I let them play only in the interests of historic preservation. It's a folkway, after all, Soule is…"

"Just what kind of game is it exactly?" Dad asked.

The librarian puffed on his pipe. "It is, gentlemen, a golfing game, but not merely so. It is also mystical, and, I hasten to add, highly addictive. Did you see the cartoon entitled *The Soule King*? That's the best depiction, I think, of the game's great frustration, and glory. In fact, that's exactly why the pastime was banned. What was intended as a pleasant distraction for the mental patients here on the Island soon introduced greater and more profound madness. It wasn't long before it had to be regulated."

"Why did the patients need a golf card game when they had a famous links right out their back door?"

"Consider what you already know, Young Jack. The weather here on Evalon is, at best, unpredictable. For months we hardly see the sun, thus the game of Soule proved a prefect surrogate for golf addicts fogged off the course. It also turned out to be especially liberating for our many patients who had sustained crippling injuries in the war and who could no longer play the game to their satisfaction. During the years Evalon was owned and operated by the U. S. military, nearly half of the patients here were classified as disabled."

"And finally, the game proved threatening in its appeal to the deadly sin of sloth itself. Why play the real game of golf, with its many physical, emotional, and intellectual demands, when you could play Soule from the comfort of your armchair? Soule proved most addictive to the trauma victims who needed a strong routine to buttress a failing mental health. Soule, a single game of which can sometimes take years, and which is always played with the same partners, seemed at first the prefect antidote for obsessive-compulsives, shizophrenics...the list goes on."

"How is it played?" Dad asked.

"With great difficulty," Augustus said, chuckling. "You mean what are the rules…? That's far from an easy matter to explain. Still, I shall do my best."

"First, each of the four members of a playing foursome describes a hole. Often, because Evalon's patients were encouraged to draw or to write as an integral part of their group therapy, the patient-members of the foursome would draw the course collaboratively, with each member responsible for the invention of four individual holes up and through hole sixteen. The final two holes—the all-important finishers—would be designed by the group as a whole, reflecting a blend of their aesthetics."

"The holes would often reflect the…"—Augustus paused, searching for the right word—"imaginative powers of our peculiar residents. Their tracks would often be fantastic…veritable heavens or hells. Some courses were laid out over rugged mountains, some down the sides of waterfalls, some following inland rivers replete with carnivorous fish, some through the shifting sands of enormous deserts. In any case, the foursome did not limit themselves to golf courses as they were in so-called real life but embraced demonic tracks as they existed in the mind's eye. In their diaries, some early players of Soule compared this initial invention stage to the first blush of romance or courtship, reporting true euphoria produced by their rapturous sketches."

"Could the holes be any length, or any par, or could they dream up those parameters, too?"

"The inventors of Soule realized their game must bear a close resemblance to the actual, and so they decreed any official Soule course must have a par of 72. Yardage, however, was up to the foursome, as, unlike the real game of golf, distance was irrelevant in Soule. This, in my opinion, was part of its genius, designed as it was for a population scarred by mayhem. In Soule, even a double amputee could, for all intents and purposes, bring a monster par 5 to its knees."

"Did the game begin, then, after the course had been drafted?"

"The game begin," Augustus intoned, "with the swearing of an oath as serious as any marital vow. Essentially, each member had to put their hand on *The Book of Soule*—more on that in a moment—and swear that they would never, under any circumstances, look at their mettle card until they had completed their round, and, second, that they would not, for any reason short of death or physical impairment, quit the game, once begun."

"Why those particular pledges?"

"Another excellent question, Robert, and one that revealed itself to me only after intense study." Augustus stopped himself and stood from his chair. "But where are my manners? I am so rarely a host I neglected to offer you two gentlemen a cup of tea. The kettle is boiling just now."

He excused himself while Dad and I stayed glued to our seats, spellbound. Augustus's room, as we looked around it in his absence, turned out to be more of a suite, and a lavishly appointed one at that. Books lined the walls, walls covered in a thick, rich velvet that held the vaguely sweet scent of pipe smoke. Pictures and paintings of the world's greatest writers decorated the walls alongside framed black and white photos of what appeared to be Evalon Island.

As cups and saucers clattered in the kitchen, we wandered around his apartment, examining the photos briefly before sitting back down for our host's return. "A spot of tea never hurts when trying to understand the esoteric game of Soule," Augustus said cheerfully. "Where was I? Oh yes, the Soule oath. The reason for the first part of the oath is self-evident once the true import of the mettle card becomes known."

"Metal card?"

"M-E-T-T-L-E, Robert, in the sense of inherent temperament, strength of character, and also, of course, the material from which golf clubs are forged. A clever play on words, that. In any case, as a condition to becoming a player, each member of a foursome was issued a mettle card by the Soule Master...the Soule Master being the high priest. Shaman-like, the Soule Master rose to his position by virtue of demonstrating unusual insight. The first Soule Master," Augustus continued, regarding us with unusual intensity, "assumed his position by having been the chief inventor of the game itself here at Evalon; his successors, as a result of having completed their round and having themselves a suitable temperament, as revealed in their mettle cards, for Soule Mastery."

The archivist sipped his tea, puckering. "The Soule Master would deal the sworn player one, or very rarely two, mettle cards to serve as an enlightened reading of that player's inner temperament, be it primarily virtuous or vice-filled. In almost every case, players would receive a single card, suggesting one true mettle. The advantage to two mettle cards, as I'm sure two such astute gentlemen as yourselves can conceive, was balance—a good card might, in theory, mitigate the effect of a poor one. In any event, the mettle card could not be looked at, under any circumstance, until the round had been completed."

"Sometimes a player would spend years completing his eighteen holes of Soule, only to turn over a mettle card which dashed his most intimate self-concept. This unmasking often proved devastating. More often than not, though, the player who completed a round completed it on the very strength of the temperament the card would, in hindsight, reveal, thus lending to the mettle card the force of fatedness. Also, it was generally, though not universally, accepted that the completion of a long and arduous round itself proved auspicious, and boded well as an indicator of one's mettle."

"And what happened if one accidentally saw their mettle card prematurely?"

"That was a very serious matter indeed," Augustus said, staring at Dad over the lip of his cup. "So far as I can determine, a virtual shunning ensued when a mettle card was prematurely revealed, especially if that revelation proved intentional. The other players, and at one time that was virtually all three hundred patients at the Institute, would socially and even physically isolate the offender, much as the Amish do in their tightly knit communities."

"So what explains the second part of the oath?"

"Ah yes, the no-quitting provision. Again, the utility of this particular clause made perfect sense. When you read further into the rules of the game, you'll note that Soule is essentially a team sport, more so than golf. Again, what could be better-suited to a generation of men who had, in war, learned the wisdom of one-for-all-and-all-for-one? They were our Greatest Generation, and they earned that reputation by being inherently team-oriented."

"Think of it this way," the librarian continued. "A game of Soule could and sometimes did last decades, with play occupying several hours of every day. So, for the same reason that marriage vows are required for a journey through thick and thin, sickness and health, they proved equally essential for a game that tried one's patience every bit as much as a marital union, if not more. Remember, in Soule you're married to three mates, not just one. And each depends on you if he hopes to finish his round. If one player were to quit, the other three members would have to begin from scratch, losing years of intimate and rather esoteric knowledge of their playing partner's habits, hopes, fears, and equally as important, their habits of play. You can imagine the devastation... comparable to a divorce only multiplied by the number of intimates involved...if three individuals, not just one, had to begin anew as a consequence of a partner's broken vow."

Dad set his teacup down. "Enlighten us as to the cards themselves."

"The cards are the game's greatest mystery. In a normal deck, of course, there are 52, but in the Soule deck the cards appear numberless. No one knows exactly how many exist, as, since the game has gone into such precipitous decline, we have only the memory of elders and the relative few cards extant to suggest their breadth. My own educated guess is that the cards number in the thousands. This abundance, I suspect, struck the inventors of the game as fitting. Just as the golfer never plays the same shot twice, metaphorically speaking he never turns over the same card twice. Moreover, the very variety of the cards is one reason that Soule, unlike poker, for example, or bridge, seems immune from the tedium that besets many games of chance, where the permutations of possibility, of chance itself, are ultimately limited by the size of the deck. In Soule, part of the pleasure of the draw, even though it might set you back in your journey toward round's end, was the wonderful whimsy and even humor of turning over a lavishly illustrated card you had never seen before."

"What was the objective of the game?"

"The object, Robert, was, as it is in many card games, to play your hand until you had no cards left."

"And at that point?"

"At that point you had completed your round and could turn over your mettle card. In a way, you had graduated, and you were rewarded with the ultimate artifact of your quest toward self-awareness … the revelation of your mettle."

"The cards, Augustus… You neglected to tell us the other suits."

"The mettle card was not a playing card, not a suit per se, as it remained face down until the round's completion. In fact, the mettle card went unseen by the player himself, but was, interestingly, revealed to the other members of the foursome from the very first play. In that way, Soule resembles Indian Poker, or, as it's better and more colorfully known, Blind Man's Bluff."

"Do you mean to tell me that your mettle card...the card that you might have to wait years to be revealed, was known to your playing partners from the very first moment...from the first tee?"

"What could be more appropriate? If golf is said to be the most revealing of games, and if the beneficiary of that revelation is the audience...the members of one's foursome or other onlookers...the ironic rules of Soule make perfect sense. In a way, one's partners, like one's real-life spouse or parents, know you better than you know yourself."

Dad nodded gravely. "The thing I have yet to understand, Augustus, is the actual mechanism by which the game is played."

"There again the cards prove crucial, Robert, for it's only in the cards, and by them, that the game exists. One way to understand the five categories of cards, the five suits as it were, is to use, as the players of Soule did, the term 'Par 5' as a memory aid. Each of the five categories, or suits, begins with a 'P,' a symmetry clearly intended to simplify an otherwise fiendishly arcane game."

The archivist took another sip of tea before launching further into his explanation. "The first suit, or deck, is the Play card, which includes the usually numbered irons, 1 to 9, the pitching wedge and the sand wedge, woods 1 through 7, and a putter. As in real golf, the player typically begins a hole by choosing what club he will play."

"The second suit, or deck, from which the player draws is Predicament. The Predicament category, again aptly named, consists of possible twists of fate that might confront the golfer in the course of his round. These might include meteorological conditions such as fog, or rain, or particular situations found on the course."

"The third suit...Potluck...is perhaps the most thrilling because, as its name implies, it can and does include anything. Potluck is said to be an endless deck. In my interviews with players of the past, I have documented more than 150 known Potluck cards signifying circumstantial dilemmas such as *Henpecked Husband, Divorce Attorney, Knee Surgery,* and *Tax Audit.* As is readily apparent, these cards included anything that might reasonably bear on a golfer's performance over the course of a life spent playing the ignominious game."

"The fourth 'P' in 'Par 5' is, arguably, the most indicative of the spiritual, nay religious, side of the game: Pantheon. These are the gods and goddesses presumed to have dominion over the game's elemental and terrestrial variables—the capricious flight of the ball, say, or conversely, its fickle lie"

Dad and I exchanged a knowing look, connecting Auggie's recounting with what we had seen in the vaults—Caspar's sketches and studies of these very deities.

"By the not-so-subtle look just now traded between father and son, my instinct tells me, Robert and Jack, that the two of you stumbled earlier this evening on your kin's drawing of these very daemons. As you saw, prominent among them were Draw and Fade, generally viewed as benign, though powerful, and Slice and Hook, darker deities whose worship among golfers is often coerced."

"Doubtless you saw the image of the transcendent Sky Ball. It is worth noting that the most powerful gods imagined by the game's designers often are portrayed with their animal familiars, animal totems symbolizing the god's special dominion. You will recall, for example, that Sky Ball is, appropriately, portrayed with a Canadian Goose, an animal known for its sustained flight. Again, there is much more to say in this realm, especially about the origin of this fourth category...whether, as in the other suits, the Pantheon was illustrated from actual firsthand witness...implying that the gods of golf are indeed very real...or if the Pantheon category is exceptional in the game of Soule as its sole—no pun intended—fiction." Augustus puffed his long-stemmed pipe. "We shall leave that question for future scholars of the game to divine."

"Lastly, we have the Providence suit, the fifth, and, quite appropriately, final category...Providence in the sense of god's guidance and in the sense of good judgment. Both meanings are, as it were, fully in play. Because the score of any given hand of five cards—referred to as a Hand-of-Five—was determined by *The Book of Soule,* Providence becomes the final factor bearing on the player's score. It is best conceived as the invisible hand guiding the shot, the condition of grace or lack thereof created by the golfer in combination with the gods. As this is an especially difficult deck to explain, allow me to illustrate."

Augustus pulled from the drawer of his coffee table a sheet of loose-leaf paper, which he handed first to Dad and which Dad passed to me. "This pictograph," Augustus continued, "is a version I traced from one of the originals in the archives. The card you have before you is *Calamity,* as illustrated by the rather precarious position in which our golfer finds his ball. Again the game's makers show their genius as well as their sense of humor. It is indeed to be caught in the jaws of a calamity to find, as the duffer depicted on the card does, his ball at rest in the gaping jaws of an alligator. Does one play it as it lies? The rules of golf make no allowance for such a ghastly predicament. This then is Providence, the work of capricious gods assigning mortal man the most unlikely circumstance to draw forth his most revealing play."

"Another of the providential images my research has unearthed is a card still more abstract than *Calamity,* though no less artful: *Perception.* The card shows a one-eyed shepherd holding his crook and, beyond, a links closely cropped by his flock. The card merits special attention for several reasons, most of all because it gives appearances of being more hermetic, more private in its signification, than the rest. It begs the question: What good is a shepherd with one good eye? And yet here again Soule seems not only to imitate life, but to transcend it. For we recall the Greek prophet Tiresias who owed his unmatched powers of perception, ironically, to his blindness. The one-eyed shepherd card is, we may be certain, deeply ironic, and, in its irony, sublimely true."

"Thus the golfer who draws the one-eyed shepherd for his Providence may either divine from that draw a certain degree of imprudence about his play...that is, what fool would trust a one-eyed shepherd with his flock...or he or she might read into their pick an extraordinary degree of irony intimating still greater powers of insight. In either case, the card player's perception has been piqued, and perhaps altered. The *Perception* card, for this very reason, exhibits greater plasticity, greater variability in its referentiality, than the others I have studied, and indeed shows up in *The Book of Soule* in many compelling combinations—sometimes weakening a hand, but more often strengthening it."

"Augustus, how then does one begin? How does the Soule player get to the first tee?"

"The game begins when the first player puts his ball in 'play' by putting down a Play card. Understand, his 'hand' is large by comparison with conventional card games. Each Soule player begins with up to 14 clubs or Play cards, and nine cards each of the other four suits, or decks...indicative of the numerological significance of nine in the game of golf...for a total opening hand of 14 plus 36, or up to 50 cards."

"The first to put his ball in play does so with a Play card of his choosing. The Predicament and Pantheon card are then supplied from the respective decks of two of his three partners. Next, the player draws his own Potluck card at random from the voluminous Potluck deck. Finally he himself draws his Providence card from the Providence deck to complete the Hand-of-Five, or 'the play'...a play begun by his own hand, altered by the addition of his playing partners' cards, and by himself completed."

"Then what?" Dad asked. "The player has five cards, but how does he know how he fared on the hole, or on the whole?"

"A delightfully bad pun, Robert. Here is where the game becomes most complicated, and where it distinguishes itself from nearly every other card game the world has ever known. To determine the outcome of the combination of intentional and providential cards making up the Hand-of-Five, the player need now consult *The Book of Soule*...a mammoth copy of which, you may have noticed, resides in Evalon's library, though the game has fallen into such disrepute few crack its spine."

"You mean the book the old men had out on the table?" I asked.

"One and the same, I'm afraid. It's a cumbersome concordance and not easy to read, but it is, I'll grant its authors, ambitious. Imagine all the mathematical combinations of cards it would have to account for given a seemingly limitless deck. Of course, here is where, once more, experience counts, just as in real golf. The seasoned player of Soule could recollect, after thousands of plays, many of the more common combinations and their scores as listed in *The Book of Soule,* thereby speeding up play among the foursome and increasing the chances that a player might, if the golf gods willed it, complete a round in as little as a few years."

"Naturally, given the difficulty of completing eighteen holes of Soule in any case, many of the hands one plays are 'whiffs,' failing to produce any stroke-inducing or hole-completing combinations as listed in the concordance. Rare indeed is the hand *The Book of Soule* rewards a hole itself...a hole being the home run of Soule. More common, but still rare, is a Hand-of-Five deemed sufficiently auspicious by the book to earn its player a stroke... the equivalent of a single in baseball. That, Robert and Jack, is another way to complete a hole...by painstakingly earning single strokes with many individual hands until one reaches the assigned par...3, 4, or 5...just as in baseball four singles, in theory, equal a run scored. Complete eighteen such holes and you've completed a round. But that, my friends, is the yeoman's path, and penny ante. Most men do not have the patience for it. As a species we prefer the home-run hitter."

I wondered if then was the right time to divulge my secret to Dad and Augustus, namely that one of the Soule cards from the geezer game in the library had fallen, undrawn, from the deck and slipped to the floor, and that I had pocketed it for safekeeping... and for historical preservation, of course.

"What about this card?" I asked, pulling the image of an angel innocently from my pocket. "What does it do?"

Augustus snatched the card from my hand, examining it greedily.

"Where did you find this?"

"The old men in the library..."

"Do you mean to tell me one of those old duffers was holding *this card?*"

"Go on, Augustus, tell us what my enterprising young son has found," Dad urged.

"This, Robert, is one of the single most valuable Providence cards in the great deck of Soule, the *Salvation* card. I heard it spoken of once but have never seen it myself...until now. My god, what a treasure!"

A cloud seemed to travel across Augustus's face then, leaving him crestfallen. "Dr. Cragg would have me fired if he knew I was allowing the last foursome on the Island to continue its game of Soule in the library, and doubly so if he knew this card had landed in their deck."

Reluctantly, it seemed, Augustus passed the *Salvation* card to father for inspection.

"Dr. Cragg, as you may know, is head golf instructor here on the Island, and, for all intents and purposes, our director and fuehrer. He's an institution here at the institution."

"Very good, Augustus." Dad shook his head appreciatively at the archivist's awful pun.

Auggie pulled a green, leather-bound volume from his shelf and handed it to me while Dad admired my angelic card. The title of Auggie's book read *On Golf and Soule*.

"Another of our exceedingly rare Evalon relics," Augustus beamed. "Only three hundred copies were ever printed, one for each of our patients back in the halcyon days of the Institute, one for each of the staff, and one for the archives."

"This was published by the Evalon Institute," Dad said, examining it. "Apparently right here on the Island."

"Dr. Cragg had the foresight to create a printing press. Marvelously useful when it came to reaching our patients with literature of use to them. Many were avid readers, and having received in-person instruction from Dr. Cragg on our links, eagerly awaited his new editions, which were themselves rare as hen's teeth. I myself had purview over the doctor's press, and so I know that beyond a few occasional pamphlets and that groundbreaking work you hold in your hands, nothing more was ever produced under his name."

"The copyright date on this, Augustus … 1945?"

"I fail to understand the significance of your observation, Robert."

Dad paced the parlor floor. "If Jack and I are to have a lesson from Dr. Cragg tomorrow, then Harlan Cragg would have to be …"

The librarian dismissed the thought with a wave of his hand. "Incredibly, dreadfully, unthinkably old. It won't pay you to do the math, Robert. But you're quite right, he is still living, and ornery as ever, I can assure you."

"It's simply not possible," Dad protested. He put his arms behind his back again, like he did on our trail walks at Grum's cabin. In Augustus's living room, in that haze of pipe smoke, surrounded by all those books, he looked like Sherlock Holmes himself. "Our Dr. Cragg would be, by conservative estimate, almost 100 years old. No one can give playing lessons at that age."

"Your logic is perfectly sound, Robert, but for one fatal flaw. You forget you are no longer on the mainland. Dr. Cragg is only the best example of a phenomenon we here call 'Evalon time.' Put simply, time moves more slowly on the Island."

"That's impossible, Augustus. I'll grant you time might *appear* to move more slowly, and that a place can become known for its distinctive rhythm—lands of manana, lands of nod. For the visitor to such places, time may seem irrelevant, often because he is in love, or he is at play, or at prayer. But he is aging at the same rate as before."

"Has Evalon taught you nothing?" Augustus exclaimed. "Perception *is* reality. If the man or the woman feels young, he or she is young. If the golfer feels powerful, he is powerful. You forget that the relativity of time and age is a fact well-accepted all over the world, though nowhere perhaps is it quite as strongly manifest as here at Evalon. Consider the more remote islands in the Japanese archipelago, where life expectancies dwarf those in the Western world."

Dad spun around on his heel, just as I'd seen him do back home in the courtroom when he was struck by an argument likely to win a jury.

"You mean to suggest, dear Augustus, that the figure in that photo on your wall, of the two young men standing beside a printing press, one distinctively mustachioed with hands awash in printer's ink, and the other beside him wearing a wool waistcoat and cravat and leaning on a golf club, is not you and Dr. Harlan Cragg circa a time period very close to the publication of the very book I now hold in my hand?"

I held tight to the *Salvation* card, awaiting Augustus's reaction.

"Bravo, Robert. Accomplished golfers are always such an observant lot. I suppose had I wished more earnestly to hide that charming bit of history, I would have removed the offending photo from the wall before you entered my chambers. But your visit tonight was unexpected, and it is rather late. Kindly forgive my negligence." He bowed ever so slightly. "And I shall try to forgive myself my carelessness."

"Yes," the archivist continued, nervously tapping a very large, bronze flowerpot with his slipper, "your deduction is correct. The picture shows one Dr. Harlan Cragg and one Augustus Repartee after the successful first printing of *On Golf and Soule*. Those were happy days indeed," Augustus said, a bit of sadness in his voice. "Your dating of the events portrayed in the photo is likewise correct."

Now I was doing the math. "That would make you ..."

"As old as Dr. Cragg? Not quite, Young Jack, but very nearly. I am exactly ten years his junior... I don't look it, wouldn't you agree?"

"Not a day over 87," Dad said, a sly smile creasing his face as he flipped through Dr. Cragg's golfing bible.

I mumbled, still disbelieving my eyes, "You don't look any older than my dad."

"I happen to think I look a few years younger than your old man," Augustus said, pretending to brush his gray-ginger locks like a teenage girl. "I attribute my preternaturally youthful looks to Evalon Time. One of several reasons why I continue to stay on this blessed, wretched, fog-enshrouded Island."

The archivist yawned then, opening his mouth wide like a lion. "I am afraid, gentlemen, as stimulating as this evening has been, that Mr. Repartee must retire. I need my beauty rest." He winked. "Robert, would you kindly return to my loving arms the very rare copy of Dr. Cragg's book you now hold in yours? I would lend it to you, but I would lose sleep over it, and I think it best that you meet the doctor without preconceived notions. He is a man to be experienced in the moment, and in no other way."

Augustus shuffled to the door, signaling our exit. A draft of refreshing, late-night air in-rushed from the hall, replacing the stale pipe smoke and philosophy that had accumulated in our hours in the archivist's chambers.

Dad shook the librarian's hand warmly, thanking him for the evening, and turned to head down the hall. "Oh, I almost forgot, Augustus. What would you have me do with the foursome in the library playing Soule?"

The librarian stretched his long arms out until they reached the very top of the door. "I suppose I don't see any harm in letting the old boys have an overnight just this once. They'll be so exhausted in the morning they'll sleep for two days straight, and I shall be able to work in peace. Sometimes it's better to let the child gorge themselves on the cookies, lest he covet them too much."

"Are you sure you don't want us to flush them out?" Dad asked, putting his hand atop my tired head. "It wouldn't be any trouble."

"Let their infantile game go on. In my frustration with those oblivious gray-hairs, even I sometimes forget theirs is the last game of Soule being played anywhere in the world. Its value to a scholar like me is priceless, even if they do prevent me seeing their hands and insist on playing in silence. They're old, old men— older than I am—and I suspect they are only trying to complete their round before ... before dark, one might say. I should do what I can to help them, even if Dr. Cragg would have me fired for my insubordination."

Augustus raised his hand to preempt our further questions. "Why, you wonder, does Dr. Cragg forbid the playing of Soule? You may have your answer straight from the horse's mouth tomorrow ... that is, if the horse doesn't bite."

And with that Augustus Repartee bid us goodnight and godspeed.

WATER HAZARD

Nine

"G'day, fellers," the old ferryman greeted us, "how was yer first day on Evalon?"

"Enlightening," Dad said, pausing to consider. "I can honestly say I learned a great deal."

"And you, lad?"

"I'm ready to golf."

"Good on ye, boy, for it's golf you'll be gettin' just now, special orders of Dr. Cragg."

Dad had made sure to set the alarm for our final day at Evalon, saying he didn't want the Brahmin showing up at our door again reeking of "be-ah."

Instead we had been woken by a call from the front desk informing us that Charles, the ferryman, would meet us at the dock. For a minute I'd thought we were being exiled to the mainland as punishment for our previous night's snooping, but Dad assured me that Charles had likely been conscripted only to carry us to our next lesson.

"It's still too foggy to hit a golf ball," I whined to our captain as he tied a second boat behind his old shrimper. Charles handed Dad and me a life jacket, just as he had on our ferry ride over.

"Not off the point, 'tisn't foggy, laddie. Where it's windy 'tisn't foggy and, bly me, it's windy out there."

Dad watched the black-bearded ferryman's actions with a mixture of concern and bemusement. "Don't you think the seas are a little rough for an excursion, Charles?"

The old boatman looked up from his rigging. "Aye, they're

plenty angry today, Master Robert. But I must do as the doctor orders."

"But we don't have to," Dad said, standing his ground. "The last thing I care to do on vacation is go to my watery grave."

"What if, Master Robert, you'd be endangering yerself and the boy by not comin' out to sea?"

"What is that supposed to mean?"

Charles heaved a heavy sigh, dropping his ropes momentarily, and turning to face us. "Dr. Cragg has ordered up for ye special the Janus Hole. 'Tis a rare privilege, a trial to test yer mettle. If I were ye, I'd take the old doc up on his offer. Ye needn't be worryin', Master Robert, I'll be right beside ye the whole time in my boat. If you and Young Jack have the slightest bit of trouble, I'll reel ye in like a load a shrimp."

"A comforting thought, Charles."

"Now if yer man enough to play the Janus Hole, hope aboard, maties."

Wordlessly, Dad and I climbed aboard the shrimp boat. I should have been terrified at the prospect, but for some nameless reason, I wasn't. It could have been that I was craving adventure, or so claustrophobic that I wanted to get off the Island at all cost. Or it might have been Charles's promise of a fogless view, but I felt certain we should go.

"Ye won't be ridin' with me s'morning, Master Robert," Charles called over cheerily. He pointed to a modified pontoon covered in artificial turf and tied up for towage behind the shrimper. "Dr. Cragg himself designed that wee vessel for the playin' of this hole 'n particular."

Dad held out his hand to help me back onto the dock and, from there, onto the tippy skiff, whose floats ran parallel down the center rather than down the sides like any pontoon I'd ever been on. The boat wobbled with my first step on deck, and doubly so with Dad's. "I wonder how Dr. Cragg would enjoy a lawsuit," Dad said, darker than I'd heard him since we'd come to the coast.

Charles shouted instructions to us over the roar of the shrimp boat's engine. "We'll be goin' to the point. When I give ye the signal of the slittin' throat I'll be cuttin' the line and ye'll be lookin' for the Janus Hole … meanin' one green in front of ye on the Island proper and another, a mirror image of the first, behind ye out on Janus Rock, out t' sea. 'Tis a double green." He winked. "I'll be cuttin' yer rope so ye'll have a clear shot from the tee. Ye'll find aboard yer wee skiff two clubs, a 4- and a 5-iron. Ye mus' trust Dr. Cragg. The old coot knows his yardages."

"Where is the tee?" Dad called after our captain.

"Yer sittin' on it!" Charles called back, opening the throttle up and taking us out to sea.

Our little skiff crashed through the surf in the wake of Charles's shrimper, skipping more than cutting through the crests. Several times the tops of smaller whitecaps sent their spray cascading onto our sea-slick deck. The old man was as nervous as I'd ever seen him, deep water being the only thing on earth that greatly afeared him.

We hugged the shore of the Island at a distance of what appeared to be no more than a 150 yards. Exactly at the point he'd promised, Charles made the signal of the slit throat, cupped his hands, and shouted something to us lost to the surf. Then he cut the rope, setting us adrift.

As the old ferryman predicted, the fog had lifted on the point, and a golf green perched atop a cliff came into view on Evalon Island. Behind Dad, further out to sea, another green emerged from the mist, this one atop a rock outcropping—the Janus Rock no doubt.

"Charles only gave us two pearls," the old man shouted to me over the roar of the sea. "Which of us should hit?"

I crouched low on the pontoon, paralyzed by the immensity of the ocean and by the sudden realization that I could not see the ferryman and his shrimper anymore.

"Jack," Dad yelled again, "you or me?"

"Both of us! But you first, into the wind, out to Janus Rock. Take the 4-iron."

Dad nodded. I'll never forget the sight of him, always so balanced and graceful, attempting to find his legs, to merely stand, on that little flatboat as it wobbled on the shoulders of the sea. Fear gripped me.

He managed to stand somehow and align himself to the green waiting atop Janus Rock. He went through his ordinary pre-shot routine, the one I'd seen thousands of times, but stopped mid-backswing, as the shifting of his weight made his end of our tippy skiff nosedive. Desperation flashed in his eyes. He attempted to squat, to lower his center of gravity, but stopped. It would only make standing upright again that much more treacherous.

"Move in … toward the center," I shouted at him. "It's the only way to balance the boat." Until then, we'd been a seesaw, Dad on one end with his 200 pounds and the force of his powerful swing, me on the other, unable to counterbalance him.

He nodded, crabbing backward with great difficulty toward the center of our sea-tossed pontoon. I did the same. Once met in the middle, we set up to our iron shots, head to head, so close we could feel the other's breath.

"Me first?" Dad had to shout his question. Around us, the ocean roiled and sizzled. The god of our giant water hazard had upped the ante.

"Both of us … at the same time. It's the only way we'll be able to swing hard enough. On the count of three ..."

I could feel the boat lurch to Dad's end as he put his weight into his shot. Remembering his three-count swing rhythm, the one I'd absorbed just by watching him hit balls back home, we finished our swings at exactly the same time. Perfectly in synch, our clubheads clanked together on their forward arc, knocking us both off balance. Dad reached out to steady me, but missed, tumbling backward to the edge of the pontoon, and then, arms windmilling, into the sea.

I'll never forget the terror of seeing him disappear beneath those waves, then the euphoria of seeing his head bob up again, buoyed by the life jacket. But the wind-driven waves were growing fiercer, and in its fear Dad's body had become heavy.

He didn't yell for help, didn't flail as you'd expect. The waves would come, wash over him, and he would reemerge, a few feet further to sea. In the seconds I stood there paralyzed, unsure what to do, it seemed as if he had surrendered himself to the waves, ruling out rescue. At a time when most men would have cried out, would have wept like a baby for salvation, my old man appeared ready to let the ocean have him.

I leapt in, into a sea that was twice as cold as my brain had reckoned, and began stroking my way toward him with all my strength. Never before in my life had I done anything—not even golf—with such purpose and urgency.

I reached Dad at exactly the moment I saw the shrimper motoring toward us through the sea spray. I held on tight, tilting his head up and out of the water until, a moment later, a rope ladder landed beside us. I grasped it with one hand and held fast to Dad with the other, until Charles, with his great, ferryman's hands, pulled Dad aboard, unconscious from the shock, or from the cold, neither of us could be certain.

"We've got to get him back to the lodge!" I screamed at the thick boatman, whose usually cheery face was painted with concern. He stumbled back to steerage and opened the throttle up.

On deck, I held my once-invincible father, the man who had never met his master, limp in my arms.

HENPECKED
HUSBAND

The Back Nine

Ten

We had had enough. We wanted off the Island.

We left the realization unspoken between us for a while, half-listening as Ava McIntosh informed us we'd be meeting with Dr. Cragg for what she called a "preliminary interview." Dad had made a quick recovery, warmed by a roaring lodge fire and Ava's able ministrations. But something had changed for us out there on the unsettled seas of Evalon, and whatever it was, it had followed us here.

Ava further promised if the fog lifted even slightly—and the forecast said it would—we would have a playing lesson with the doctor himself...a rare treat, she assured us.

"I'll be drivin' y'all down to his cottage on the far side of the Island," she dripped. "Actually" she corrected herself. "I'll be dropping y'all off at the back gate. He's not only banned Soule, but golf carts, too." Her eyes twinkled with mischief. "But what he doesn't know surely won't hurt him."

"Ava," Dad asked quietly. "What is the point of the Janus Hole?"

"I ought to leave the explanation to the doctor," she replied, choosing her words carefully, "though it's impossible to know whether he'll mention it. He can be a man of few words, or he can be a man of many. It depends on his mood."

Dad frowned deeply at Ava's dodge-of-an-answer. Our lady pro, sensing the grave mood his sea-spill had put us in, quickly relented. "The Janus Hole," she sighed, "is one of the doctor's most rigorous pre-examinations. Years ago, he insisted that Jake

107

and I do a better job of weeding our students. To assist us in that process he developed the Janus Hole, so named after the Roman goddess of doors and entries. When the citizens of Rome portrayed Janus, she appeared in profile, a mirror image with two-faces—one looking forward, one looking back."

The old man rubbed his hands together for warmth. "So the challenge of the Janus Hole is the challenge of a puzzle and a Zen koan all at once: How does one play two holes simultaneously?"

"The challenge, Robert, is threefold. First, is the courage requisite to take to the sea in the skiff. Most of our pupils refuse. The second challenge is the riddle posed by the boat itself, which Dr. Cragg engineered only to support the dynamic weight transfer of a golf swing if that swing was properly counterbalanced by a shot from the opposite side in the opposite direction. Janus is only Janus, after all, if she looks both ways equally."

"The third challenge lies in executing the shot under such unforgiving conditions as y'all faced today. To hit those two greens, simultaneously, from a floating tee at a distance of some 180 yards is no small feat, gentlemen. And, of course, no small amount of luck."

"We never verified our shots made the greens," Dad pointed out, arms folded firmly across his chest. "We've only Charles's word, and I don't know how he could know, given that he remained on his shrimper the whole time."

"Charles has his ways," Ava said, somewhat mysteriously. "And he's a straight-shooter, as we say here on the Island. Besides, don't forget our lesson from yesterday."

"The dream of the shot is the shot." Dad repeated the words robotically, his tone this time indicating he was less than convinced.

"In sum, y'all performed beautifully this morning—beautifully enough to earn Dr. Cragg's invitation to his cottage… And that is where I must take y'all now. The doctor expects punctuality of everyone but himself."

But Dad wasn't budging. "What kind of a doctor jeopardizes the safety of a young boy and his father, Ms. McIntosh? I understand his need to test his students' mettle, but to endanger them in the process is unforgiveable. We signed up for a golf academy, not a survival course."

"Sometimes they're one and the same," our lady pro replied, watching us closely. "Robert, I understand your anger. Even Jake and I have, in the past, requested the doctor reconsider the Janus Hole. But he is not a man given to compromise, which is precisely what has allowed him to transform the games, indeed the very souls, of thousands of students and patients, stretching back many, many years, and the reason why, in the end, I continue to work for him. His uncompromising stance is an integral part of his method."

"Ava," Dad said gently, for women always seemed to bring the gentleness out in him, "Have you ever stopped to wonder whether your teaching might better flourish under a different kind if tutelage? The doctor's uncompromising method is an old one, true, and history may reveal it to be an effective one, but it is not the only one."

Ms. McIntosh smiled wryly at the old man's observation, as if she had rehearsed the same argument to herself many times before. "You almost met your end today, Robert…"

"Too true."

"And have you considered your end before? Ever imagined what it would look like, how it would feel?"

Dad glanced over at me, clearly unsure if, and how, he should answer in my presence.

"Of course I have, Ms. McIntosh."

"And what did you conclude?"

"That I would accept my death when and how it came."

"And would you say that realization, that morbid thought, has enlightened you in any particular way?"

"More than any other single thought to which I've given my sincere attention."

"Why is that, do you suppose?"

"Because everything is conjecture until a man considers his own death, contemplates meeting his maker. If a man can live with that reality, if he can really feel it, he comes not to fear the world, but to advance in it, and sometimes through it, all other fears being judged, in the end, as lesser. In effect, he is living two lives, one in the now, on earth, in his body, and one in the hereafter."

"What if I told y'all that is exactly why the doctor designed the Janus Hole as he did, and why for him golf is not merely a game, but a mortal danger? If golf is truly a transcendent pursuit, if it really possesses the ability to reveal a man's soul, his mettle, it could not be otherwise… That's why I continue to teach here at Evalon, not because there aren't other choices, but because I have come to believe in the sanctity of making that one big choice—to enable life by embracing death. That's why I've come here, and I think that is why y'all have come to me, and, by extension, to the doctor."

The old man considered Ava's words in total silence, as if caught in his own tortured, internal debate, and then, looking at me intently, he found the words that would change our lives forever: "Very well then, we shall go and see the doctor."

CONFUSION

Eleven

As promised, Ava dropped us off at a stone wall into which was set an iron gate. Over the gate hung a sign notched in weathered wood: *Beware Ye Who Enter. Golf is a Dangerous Game.*

"Not very welcoming, is it?" Ava's pretty mouth formed a frown. "We've asked the doctor to change it many times. In any case, here is where I must leave y'all. Follow the stone path down to the house and knock once."

Dr. Harlan Cragg's cottage sat just far enough back from a small jetty to protect if from the wrath of the sea, but close enough to make a storm surge an ever-present threat. In its remoteness there on the edge of the Island away from the lodge, it looked like a lighthouse keeper's quarters, lonely yet strangely inviting.

Dad led the way through a small, overgrown rose garden to a wooden door where he knocked once, following Ava's instructions.

"Come in, for Christ's sake!" a voice from inside screamed. "Jesus, do I have to open the goddamned door for you?" Dad arched an eyebrow at me, as if to say, *Here goes nothin', son.*

We opened the door to a large living room full of rustic charm and a roaring fire. On the walls hung golfing memorabilia in a manner similar to our Dark Horse room at the lodge. Sheepskin rugs dotted the stone floor, softening the primitive surroundings.

A white-haired man with sharp, angular features sat facing us in a rocking chair. He wasn't especially tall or imposing, as I had imagined, but compact and full of barely contained energy. His eyes, set behind a thick pair of glasses, followed our movements intently. He did not rise to meet us. Instead Dad and I sat down, at his motioning, on the sofa nearest him.

"To what do I owe this particular pleasure?" the doctor inquired after an uncomfortably prolonged silence.

"A friend of ours saw your academy's advertisement in a publication," Dad began.

"A more enlightened soul would term it an *invitation,* not an *advertisement,* Mr. Johannes," the doctor scoffed. "An advertisement, as I would have assumed a man of your education to understand, is sent out indiscriminately. An invitation is dispatched to a targeted few. What I sent was an invitation. Besides, I well know how you got here. Let me repeat the question: *To what do I owe this pleasure?"*

Dad sat silent for a moment, pondering. "You owe this pleasure to a series of events too many and too varied to describe. To fate, I suppose."

"Do you believe in fate, Mr. Johannes?"

"Call me Robert, Doctor."

"I shall call you whatever I like," Cragg snapped, raising his voice sharply. "Answer the question. Do you believe in fate?"

"I do, but then again I don't."

"Explain yourself." The doctor leaned back in his rocking chair, making a temple with his fingers.

"I accept it and I reject it all at once."

"Now we're getting somewhere. Go on."

"It wouldn't be proper to put a percentage on it," Dad explained. "For example, to say that man's ultimate end is half his own doing and half the result of an unseen force…the will of the gods…fate if you will."

"Gods?"

"I use 'gods' as an expression only, Doctor, to put a face on the unknowable, on chance."

"I dare say the gods would object to such a downgrading."

"What I mean to say," Dad clarified, "is that fate and man's will … his volition … operate concurrently and reciprocally."

"I knew there was a reason I asked you here," the doctor enthused. "Boy," he groused at me, "look sharp over there! This isn't middle school."

The fire, my fatigue after the drama of the Janus Hole, the low rumble of the two voices exchanging volleys … My eyes had grown heavy.

"How can it be that will and fate are coequal, Mr. Johannes? There cannot be two one hundred percents, can there? That's a logical impossibility."

"Unless they overlap so closely and so seamlessly it's impossible to tell where one begins and where the other ends. It's fluid, wouldn't you agree, Doctor?"

The question appeared to perturb our host. "We're not talking about what *I* think, Mr. Johannes, we're talking about what *you* think. Kindly refrain from your juvenile line of rhetorical questioning. So, since you are here to enroll in a golf academy…"

"Coulda fooled me," I muttered under my breath.

"What's that, young man?"

"Nothing."

"That's what I thought… Thus applying your theory, Mr. Johannes, to the game of golf, which I think we can agree is no different than the game of life, you're telling me that the fate of the ball is in fact the equal and reciprocal intention of god and man, a cosmic accident and a sublimely orchestrated execution, in equal measure, all at once?"

"Just so," Dad said.

"And if that is true, why do million of golfers spend all of their energies practicing the mechanics of the game rather than perfecting their methods of devotion, of supplication, even of sacrifice?"

"A good question, Doctor."

"And here's another: Why does the golfer attempt to make a god of himself rather than spend his devotion in contemplation of higher powers?"

"I suspect because he is sure of his own existence, but not of the existence of the gods to which he would be appealing."

"Even though his whole, wretched, repressed golfing life he feels their divine presence, intuits them as deeply as he does the existence of his own soul? And yet the fool golfer comes to focus only on those aspects of the game he can control, leaving the rest to the very gods he is unable to acknowledge. And in so doing he willingly cedes his own miraculous powers of creation to a pantheon he scarcely knows exists and is often quite helpless to imagine."

"Here you imply the golfer's belief is almost delusional, whereas before…"

"I am aware, Mr. Johannes, of the apparent contradiction in my sentiments, which may be summarized thusly: Golf, a game demanding great will and volition, requires the golfer make of himself a god at the same time that it continually undermines the creation of his false, egotistical idol with countless acts of chance and caprice."

The doctor stopped to rub his glasses on his wool overshirt before continuing. "In this light, your supposition of two one hundred percents, waxing and waning all the time, adding up, at any given moment, not to two hundred percent, as one might expect, but to one hundred percent, is actually quite compelling."

"But suppose," the doctor added, arguing with renewed intensity, "that man is only a product of the imagination of his divinity, not the other way around. Suppose the golfer is dependent, for his very anemic swings at grace, on the golfing gods. Better golf, then, would be akin to better religion, to better faith. The swing would become a prayer, and the prayer a sacred intention." The doctor paused for effect. "What is your intention, Robert?"

"My intention for what, Doctor?"

"Your intention for golf?"

"You mean why do I play?"

"I mean," the doctor said with still greater emphasis, "what do you *intend* by your play?"

"I suppose my intention is a graceful, rhythmic swing…one that brings me pleasure, and pleasure to those around me."

"I asked about your intention, Robert, not your method." Dr. Cragg's tone was stern.

"I see…" Dad mumbled, deep in thought. "My intention, then, if you put it that way, would be peace. Yes, my intention by the playing of golf is peace."

"Everlasting peace?"

"Momentary peace."

"And if you could achieve truly everlasting peace through golf, would you accept it, Robert, as the very utmost of your intentions, the purest fulfillment of your wish?"

"I would," Dad said, serious as a vow.

"Then you would have found a golfing heaven, a Nirvana. And you would have found it, like the whirling dervishes of old, by dancing, for a golf swing is nothing more and nothing less than a dance."

"True peace achieved through golf would indeed be heaven, Doctor."

"And you, Young Jack," the old man said, turning on me without warning, "what is your intention when you play the greatest of games?"

"My intention is to win," I said slowly.

"Delightful!" the doctor exclaimed, clapping like a child. "A warrior. What then is your method, soldier?"

"My method," I said, repeating his question aloud to buy time, "is to hit challenging golf shots in competition. That's the only way you can really test..."

"Your mettle."

"I wasn't going to say that exactly, sir."

"But that is what you intended to say?"

"Yes."

"Here I have before me a father and son, both talented golfers, one of whom is a peace-lover while the other is a warrior. One dances while the other one thrusts. What am I to make of this?"

The doctor placed his palm on his clean-shaven cheek in thought. "What defines winning, Jack?"

"Beating everyone else... all your competitors."

"What about yourself. Are you one of your competitors?"

"I guess so."

"So it is possible to win, in effect, by triumphing over your-self at the same time you are triumphing over others? But what if, young man, your competitors are just illusions, just projections, and it is yourself, and yourself only, you are competing against. Then would *defeating* yourself constitute a win?"

"It would," I said.

"And would you be at peace then, to use your father's words?"

"I would... temporarily."

"There, gentleman, is where your philosophies, so different on the surface, join at the hip like Gemini twins. You seek the same end by radically different methods. You are both predisposed to accept only the idea of a temporary victory, a temporary peace.

Naturally, of the two, it is the older man who is at least willing to grant the notion of an everlasting peace."

"Tell me, have the two of you, outside of the Janus Hole, ever played golf together, as a team, in effect forcing your conflicting methods into direct confrontation?"

"Not as much as we should, Doctor. I'm afraid that's my fault," Dad said, casting his eyes downward.

"And why is it your fault, Robert?"

"Because a father is supposed to take the initiative to play with his son."

"That may be so," the old pro said. "But surely you have played an actual competitive round together at least once."

"Just once," Dad conceded, swallowing hard. "We were… unable to finish."

"For god's sake why?"

"Because I quit."

"Quit? My heavens, Robert, you don't strike me as the quitting type. Something extraordinary must have happened to cause you to stop." The doctor turned to me. "Young Jack, have you any idea what that extraordinary something might have been?"

I had the distinct feeling that Cragg knew much more about us than he had been letting on. He seemed to be staring into our very souls.

"We quit because we got…impatient," I confessed.

"Come now, your father here would not quit because he grew *impatient,*" Cragg said. "I am only getting to know him, mind you, but he seems a very patient man, perhaps patient to a fault. No, there must be something else…"

"And also," I added, a knot growing in my stomach. "I hit him."

"*You hit him,*" the doctor repeated matter-of-factly, and then

119

again, with a slightly different intonation and more to himself. *"You hit him."*

"That is a rather serious matter, Jack. But it's not uncommon for sons to take a swing at their fathers, if the two love one another sufficiently to come to either physical or verbal blows. Tell me, Robert, what did you do to so provoke your son's ire?"

"We were playing a best shot at the time and I"—Dad stopped, hanging his head—"failed to take the best interests of the team to heart."

"What did you do exactly that angered the boy?"

"I hit several consecutive shots in the water while going for the green in two on a par five."

"I presume the lad wanted you to lay up?"

"The problem," Dad said, making a pained, almost furtive glance in my direction, "was not only that I hit three in the hazard, but that one of those shots I struck at...at Jackie...while he attempted to obstruct."

"Thus risking the life of the young man you yourself imbued with life." The old doctor shook his head.

"I knew I wouldn't hit him," Dad mumbled.

"Just as you *knew* that every one of those three balls would not land in the water? Just as you *knew* that the gods of golf would exercise their willful percentage and save your son from wayward parentage? Correct me if I'm wrong, Robert, but I thought we had established that the gods of golf have their own volition, and, consequently, that had they wished your son to be struck down at the hands, or by the club, of his own father, they would have made it so regardless of your talent. You're caught in your own argument, Mr. Johannes."

"And I call myself a lawyer." Dad chuckled to himself. "You're right, Doctor."

"Now tell me why you did this extraordinarily nonsensical thing. Why did you hit those three inane shots in the water?"

"In part to show Jackie that winning isn't everything. And in part, as I told him, because I knew I had a better shot in me."

"Alas, the deepest motivation comes out last, as always." The doctor slapped his knee to punctuate his point. "There is where you were staying true to your creed...achieving a private peace... and your son likewise staying true to his...conquering the competition. It's no wonder you came to blows. And yet, as we've already seen, you both sought the same end. And somewhere in the events precipitating that injudicious shot played within a hair's breadth of your son, the very flesh of your flesh, must have been the demonic will of the gods of golf...Slice, I should think, given the nature of the offense that brought you to blows and the shape of that third, ill-fated shot."

The doctor poured himself a small glass of what Dad later revealed was whiskey. He returned to his chair renewed, licking his lips.

"Though I have never had a child of my own, I speak from experience when I speak of paternal love that leads to perdition." The doctor settled into his chair, his voice mellowing as the whiskey began to work. "During the war, a prodigiously talented golfer came to our veteran's hospital for a simple but nonetheless delicate surgery. He had what was then considered a minor injury, a shrapnel wound to the leg, and, thanks to our surgeons and nurses, he was up and golfing on the Evalon links in no time. Not just golfing, mind you, but playing the game with a freedom and daring and power never before witnessed."

Dad and I traded glances, excited at the revelation we expected would soon be ours. The doctor continued. "I soon realized I had stumbled into the perfect poster child for my patients, many of whom were too deep in self-pity and limitation to even attempt the game, much less excel at it. It's true that my shining exemplar's wounds were less serious than many others, but the principle held. They could heal themselves, to some small or large degree, if only they would try."

"And this golfer's name?" Dad asked expectantly.

"It's a name I have great difficulty uttering, even to this day."

"Please, Doctor."

"Willy...Willem Grum. His father designed these very links."

Of all the surprises awaiting Dad and me at Evalon, this was perhaps the greatest. We had both dared to anticipate in the doctor's lengthy preamble about a talented golfer the naming of Caspar, our kin, the one who had penned those magnificent drawings in the Witness Room.

Instead, the good doctor had just informed us that Old Man Grum, that perfect toad of a man, had been the most heavenly golfer Harlan Cragg had ever seen.

"What about Caspar...Caspar Johannes?" Dad asked.

"A true visionary, our Caspar, and a fine golfer, too...though he was no Willem." Sensing our disappointment, the old psychologist hastened to continue the story. "Here is where Caspar, your father, enters my story, Robert. He too was here recovering from war injuries...injuries of a more psychological nature. Under my care, Caspar prospered, and I soon cleared him to return to his family, a wife and young son. That son must have been you." The doctor waited for Dad's acknowledgement before proceeding. "Caspar thrived here. He was an intellectual as well as an imaginer. As he progressed through his treatments, he was soon serving as my unofficial assistant, so adept had he become at internalizing my own psychological method. And I...how could I not avail myself of his services? He proved to be the perfect translator of my message and my method…a psychologist's dream. He had at his disposal nearly all of the knowledge I had gained in my practice and all of my university studies, but, in the eyes of my patients, he was still 'one of them' and thus to be trusted in a way they would never trust their physician."

"I dare say the two of us became a little drunk with one another's company, flush with the prospect of golf as a means of therapy, of healing. And when Willem came along, the trinity felt complete. Caspar and I had been working on a game that would simulate the healing powers of golf for the infirm—a game so evocative of the actual that it offered many of the same satisfactions without the physical demands."

"Caspar called it *Soule,* after the Dutch name for an alleged forerunner of golf, and, naturally, for the metaphysical double entendre it offered. Your father, Robert, had created a game that indeed seemed ancient, and dangerous. It felt older indeed than golf itself, and every bit as addictive. In fact, Caspar and I copublished our findings in the top medical journal of its day to great acclaim from my colleagues." The warmth of the reminiscence seemed to light our host from within, but the effect proved fleeting. As quickly as it had brightened, his tone darkened again.

"As often happens, Caspar and I took our discoveries one step too far, much to Willy's detriment. Poor Willem proved the perfect foil for our increasingly emboldened experiments. He was simple of mind without being stupid; rationale without being unimaginative. His temperament was slow and even. And best of all, though his was a mild disposition, a fierce competitive fire burned within."

"In our too-short time together, I entertained many psychological explanations for Willem's phenomenal competitiveness. I speculated he wished to supplant his father, a noted golf course architect. Or perhaps because he had survived the injuries of war, his was a simple over-compensation for the feelings of powerlessness he had known."

"In the time I knew him, good Willem Grum was willing to try anything to improve his virtuoso abilities. He took to club-making, setting up his own shop in the shed behind this very cottage, crafting clubs custom-fit to match his powerful game."

"At the same time that Willem was fashioning a flawless swing, Caspar was inventing, and illustrating himself, with assistance from hand-picked understudies among our patients, a fantasy game imbued with an almost occult power."

"The two men seemed fated to join forces. In effect, Caspar sought to modulate his prototype cards to the unself-conscious, virtuoso game of golf as Willem played it, just as a musician might pitch-match a note he envied in another's composition. Prior to every shot Willem hit in the year it took to develop a fully workable version of Soule, Caspar would turn over the five suit cards required for a Hand-of-Five. Caspar's obsessive-compulsiveness served him well at this task, as he documented every hand he played, calibrating it with every swing Willem took. After a season of such fine-tuning, it was as if the cards had become Willem's game and Willem's game, Caspar's set of cards."

"Well into their second year of practiced calibration, Caspar made a great leap. He began to use the cards in a predictive fashion, so that before Willy had even addressed his shot, his partner had turned over the cards that would, in theory, reveal the fate of the ball unstruck. It was as if the gods of golf had found a vehicle through which to reveal their whims."

"At first Willem was excited by the prospect. Here was an advantage over the professionals he hoped one day soon to challenge. If he knew in advance where his shot might land or what mischief might be played with it by the gods, he could simply alter his play preemptively and, in so doing, become a true maestro."

"All of our hopes and fears came to a head one cold, overcast day in 1946, when Willem, who had stayed on as head pro at the Evalon links at my invitation, and Caspar, who, by his own choice had forsaken his family to remain on the Island and develop the game of Soule, met for what was to be the final trial run before Willem made an attempt to qualify as a professional and Caspar to market to hundreds of thousands of war-wounded the magic he had invented."

"They met at the ocean hole, the very same whose green you, Young Jack, played to earlier this morning while your father struck his remarkable shot to Janus Rock. The eighth was and is the most difficult on the links—an unforgiving drive through a grove of cypress to a devilishly downhill shot through a chute of trees to a green perched on a promontory hard on the sea. On the tee, Caspar drew *3-iron* for the Play card… Willy hit a 3-iron. Caspar drew *Stymie* for the second card, the Predicament. Indeed when Willy crested the hill to find his tee ball, he found it obstructed by the trunk of a massive cypress… stymied, just as Caspar's pick had foretold."

"Next Caspar pulled the Potluck card, *Unfinished Business,* and from the Pantheon deck, the god *Hook,* a she-demon that had plagued Willem his whole golfing career and Caspar, too, who had sketched the vixen as he battled her on these very links. With great trepidation, for he knew the cards thus far boded ill, Caspar Johannes drew the Providence card: *Calamity.* The draw was a singularly inauspicious one, and Caspar knew it, advising Willy to take an unplayable lie and drop within two club lengths of the massive trunk."

"But Willy was having *the round of his life*… an interesting expression, that...and playing up the eighth he stood at a record five under par. He could not justify a penalty stroke that would leave him with, at best, a bogey. So he disregarded Caspar's powerful cards for the first time in many months, testing an earth-shaking hypothesis all his own: in effect, did Willy's play make the cards or did the cards make Willy's play? Willem took out a 5-iron, the club he had forged in his own shop, and set up for a punch shot recovery he hoped would leave him no more than a chip to the green."

"When he swung, as the cards had foretold, calamity struck. His iron snapped as it contacted the mighty cypress trunk that had stymied him, sending the rogue clubhead first into the tree and then back upon poor Willem. The blade struck him squarely in the left eye, a devastating blow that caused him to stagger back into his dear friend's arms, howling."

"Caspar brought him to this very cottage, where I quickly attended to my star pupil, putting cold compresses on the eye while Caspar fetched the surgeon on-call at the hospital. The results of the surgery proved unimpressive, and the wound slow to heal. Willy was forced to wear a bandage over his left eye...the eye most essential to good golf."

"Caspar and I accompanied him months later when, on these very links, he attempted his first golf shots after removing the patch. All of us were filled with the highest hopes while simultaneously harboring the deepest doubts. And while Willy could still hit the ball well, it was clear from that afternoon and others that followed that any hope he had of turning professional had been dashed."

"As you can imagine, Robert, your father was beside himself with guilt, convinced that his own draw of the cards had been responsible for Willem's cosmic misfortune. Caspar ranted and raved and cursed the gods for the devil-game they had visited upon him. He began having visions of alarming lucidity, many of them of golf's darkest deities. When the phantasms appeared before him, he drew them, as I had always recommended, as a way of externalizing the demons. Our archivist, Augustus Repartee, has preserved many of his renderings. Most entered the Pantheon deck of Soule itself, so vivid and visceral did they prove."

"At the same time that Willem's fortunes had turned tragically for the worse, the game his good friend and companion had created, Soule, had caught on like wildfire at what by that time had become the Evalon Institute for the Mentally Insane. Tournaments involving hundreds of patients were held in the Great Hall. Caspar became revered and even feared for having invented such a dreadfully engrossing pastime, and his fawning peers declared him the first Soule Master against his will."

"What initially proved to be a great boon to our patients... restoring health and vigor virtually overnight, giving them reason, in many cases, to live...soon turned disastrous. Psych nurses began reporting increased incidences of sleepwalking, night terrors, delirium tremens, grown men crying out in their sleep in a way they hadn't since returning from the bloody trenches of Europe. Blood pressures rose. Rates of depression skyrocketed."

"As the chief psychologist, I myself noted increased incidences of schizophrenia, delusional behavior, general mania. More troubling still, Caspar, my dear friend, slipped into a madness of his own making. Though he himself did not play the game, he fell into a mania of work attempting to keep up with the demand for new cards, cards that he drew directly from his own troubled psyche, and which, for their very power, depended on his inner turmoil. Every new god or goddess he envisioned and recorded fueled the Soule players' need for more and better, until poor Caspar finally suffered a breakdown—an eventuality, as a friend, I had warned him of but felt powerless to prevent."

"And that is when the Evalon Island trinity…Willem, Caspar, and I…fractured. Disgruntled and depressed, his hopes of turning pro dashed, Willem took the ferry back to the mainland, leaving behind a rueful note advising of his return to his family's traditional profession of shepherding."

"Caspar became a patient once more at what had become, after the government sale of the property, the Evalon Institute for the Mentally Insane. Due to an obvious professional conflict, I could never again be his chief psychologist, though I would always be his friend. He made good progress after his breakdown but proved perpetually haunted not only by Willem's accident, but by the specter of death itself. He never returned to his family."

The doctor paused, looking almost tenderly at Dad, the flames leaping from the fireplace appearing to moisten Cragg's eyes.

"Caspar had drawn his own mettle card in the early stages of perfecting Soule, and it had been a card of endings, showing a flag on the 18th green and a solemn crowd observing a profound silence. Though, in another's eyes, the card would have intimated a gallery revering a fine play on the home hole, the ever-impressionable Caspar interpreted his mettle as the death card. He spoke of his own misgivings about his mortal fate many times to Willy and me."

"Despite my best efforts, the great Caspar Johannes managed to hang himself in his room, and, in so doing, turn his mettle card and his calamitous experience with Willem into a tragically self-fulfilling prophecy."

The grizzled old doctor lifted his eyeglasses to rub his face with a handkerchief. Had he shed a tear, or was he merely, in that sauna of a cottage, wiping the sweat from his brow? "I am sorry most of all for you, Robert, who never came to know him, and sorry for your kin. He was a brilliant man...compassionate, creative, a luminary in every sense of the word. He was much beloved by everyone here, everyone save himself."

Dad removed his handkerchief from his pocket and dried his own tears. I had never seen him cry, not once, and the sight made me tender toward him. I hugged him with all the force a thirteen-year-old boy musters when he sees an adult he loves suffering an inexplicable pain.

Dad looked at Cragg evenly for a long time before he spoke. "The tale itself, though a painful one for a son to hear is, for me, live-giving. I appreciate your befriending my father, and making his years at this place as good as they could possibly be. I miss him."

"Come," Dr. Cragg said, slapping both his bony knees this time, "we have been sitting longer than I had intended, and longer than is good for us. We're forecast to have a break in the weather soon, and I want to be ready when it comes. You shall have a playing lesson with me on the Links of Evalon. In the meantime, let me make us some tea and toast, and let us practice some of the more basic elements of the game away from this dreadful weather."

129

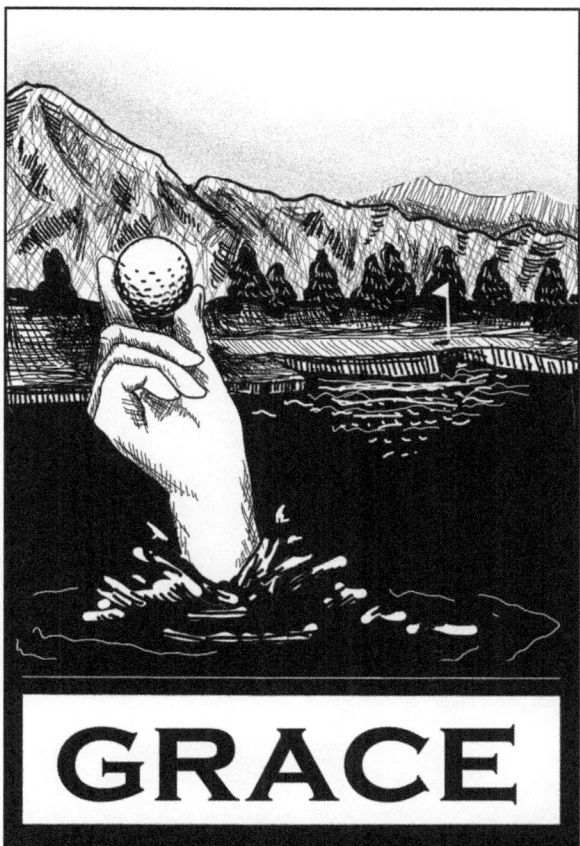

GRACE

Twelve

The doctor rose with surprising agility, bidding us be seated at the kitchen table while he ferried three plates of toast, butter, and jam over to us. On his last trip, he delivered three cups of tea and a small deck of cards bearing the insignia of Evalon.

"Robert...Jack," he said, "I am going to do something with you today that I have not done in decades of teaching, not since the earliest days, in fact. You must promise me that what transpires at this table will not be shared with anyone at the lodge— not Ms. McIntosh, not Mr. Jacobsen, not Mr. Repartee. Am I understood?" Dad and I nodded solemnly, picking at our slightly burnt toast.

"We are, gentlemen, going to play a round of Soule." The doctor raised his hand for calm. "But not without first taking all due precautions. We will not play a full deck. We will not play all of the suits. And, most importantly, we will not swear the oath. Still, be advised, these cards hold great power, not least because they were designed and invented by your own kin."

"Put simply," the doctor intoned, "they are dangerous, which is why I banned the game of Soule from the Island decades ago. I would have ended the games already in progress, too, but the results, psychologically speaking, would have been far too devastating. We did not then have half the staff required to treat the suffering of the players whose rounds would have been cut short. Blood oaths would have had to have been suspended, mettle cards prematurely revealed. It would have constituted an unspeakable trauma."

133

"I am," the doctor continued, reading our faces, "given to understand that there is one remaining game being played at the lodge by a group of gentlemen whose tenure is long-standing. They are dreadfully poor players, and miserably unlucky. Still, perhaps because of their pathetic incompetence, they are entitled to complete their round. And because they are the last, and there is no other game to join, when one is through, all will be through. And that will be a glorious day, one I have awaited for decades... Speak now, then, if you do not wish to continue with our Soule trial. I would not think less of you."

"Jack." Dad turned to me. "You know it's perfectly okay not to play, don't you?"

"I do," I said. "And you, too?" He nodded.

"Bravo, gentlemen. I pegged both of you as the bravest of souls, just like Caspar."

"Despite its many liabilities," the doctor began as he dealt Dad and me a modified hand of 27 cards, nine from each of three decks, "Soule remains the best possible training for a bona fide game of golf. This I begrudgingly acknowledge. It better simulates the magic, and the fatedness, of the game than any technique I have yet come across."

Cragg folded his arms on the table, looking from Dad to me and back again. "I myself will draw the cards in an attempt to mitigate whatever influence they may have on you. We will play together, in a manner of speaking, each of you giving your input on the modified hand we have been dealt. Our skeleton hand shall consist of nine cards representing each of three suits... Predicament, Potluck, and Pantheon. I have also improvised for our trial a fourth deck from which we will draw at random a series of challenges to be met with our existing 27 cards. Again, I repeat, we will not be playing by the official rules of Soule, nor will we be keeping score. This is merely a scrimmage undertaken for the express purpose of familiarizing you with the forces that bear upon the game and preparing you for your playing lesson to follow. Gentlemen, are you ready to approach the first tee?"

Dad and I signaled our approval, transfixed already by the number and variety of cards the good doctor had turned over.

"Let us assume," the doctor said, "that we are playing the first hole at Evalon, an uphill par 4 that heads inland, toward the lodge, doglegging slightly right. The hole presents no special difficulty architecturally, though the fairway is tight and the green is guarded by deep bunkers left and right. Further, let us assume that I draw…as I shall now do…a Predicament card showing, *Errant Bounce,* and a Potluck showing *Crosswinds.* From your given hand, which Pantheon card would you play assuming this draw? Jack, the youngest, goes first. Examine the cards carefully, boy, and pick the one that announces its rightness to you, the one that belongs to be."

Dr. Cragg leaned back in his chair while I weighed the options in my first ever hand of Soule. Should I meet the difficult draw with the card labeled *Knockdown Shot, Running Draw,* or *Sweet Spot?* Any one would do. I knew I didn't want *Sky Ball* in a wind as fierce as the cards foretold, nor did I want *Hardpan Lie* if I had drawn an errant bounce. After much consideration, I selected *Sweet Spot,* figuring that a well-struck tee-ball stood the best chance of staying in the fairway, thereby leaving me an approach to the green.

"A reasonable choice," Cragg said when finally I laid my fingers on the card of choice and played it. "In an official game of Soule, we would be playing with a Hand-of-Five, one of all five suits, two of which you would depend on your playing partners to contribute. Finally, when your Hand-of-Five was assembled, you would consult *The Book of Soule,* hoping against hope that your unique combination of cards...your inimitable play...had completed a hole or, more likely but still exceedingly rare, that your play counted as a stroke toward the hole's posted par. Already, you note how infinitely complicated the game is, and how impossible to simulate. That reminds me, I neglected to tell you about these two cards." The doctor paused, pushing across the table the two remaining face-downs he had dealt...one for Dad and one for me.

"Jack!" the doctor bellowed as I began, reflexively, to turn my card over. "You mustn't reveal a mettle card during a round in progress, not even in the midst of a trial such as ours! That, my young friend, was a very close shave. Never trifle with fate, even in adulterated form."

"And now," our host said, calming himself once more, "we turn to the father. Robert, do you share your son's choice of a Pantheon card on the first hole, given the limited number of choices represented by our sample hand?"

"I...I would be tempted to play *Running Draw.*"

"You needn't be *tempted* by it, Robert," Cragg scolded, resuming the crotchety tone with which he had greeted us. "You would play *Rolling Draw,* then? I presume because it represents a shot-maker's selection, the theory being there is more artistry in keeping the ball below the wind while holding it simultaneously against it then simply, as Young Jack has done, hitting the ball solidly and letting the crosswind and the bounce take it, no matter how well-struck, where they will. Here again, the differences between father and son reveal themselves in a most interesting way. And yet I can see that both of you deeply respect the other's play, so much so, in fact, that having seen your partner choose an alternate route, you are tempted to choose his play as your own."

"Now then," the doctor continued, "we face the approach shot on the opening hole. Once again, I will draw the Predicament card, which this time reveals *Hanging Lie,* and Potluck, which, fortunately for us, shows *Fairway in Regulation.* Again, which of the gods or goddesses in my hand will you petition? Play away, Robert."

"If I'm in the fairway with an uneven lie under a heavy crosswind, I would definitely choose *Knockdown Shot.*"

"And you, Young Jack?"

"I would choose *Running Draw.* If the shot's uphill like you said, then a knockdown would just land on the upslope and stop."

"The young master makes a good point, Robert."

"Yes, he does," Dad said, tipping his cap to me. "Although *Running Draw* is dangerous. It's difficult to control under the best circumstances."

"Right you are," the old doctor said, chuckling, clearly relishing our debate. "Now, were we playing a regulation game of Soule, you would of course make several plays with your putter, choosing from a separate and equal putting Pantheon, a group which includes deities such as *Yips, Flips, Chili Dips, Power Lips, Texas Wedge, Cellophane Bridge, Hit It, Alice,* and the rest of the colorful and often tragicomic divinities of the flat stick."

"But because I note it brightening outside and surmise our much-anticipated, albeit brief, window of playable weather has arrived, I am going to draw from the deck a Providence card. Again, in a sanctioned game, this would be the last card drawn to complete a Hand-of-Five. Since were are, in a manner of speaking, playing alternate shot, I will select our shared Providence for the hole."

Cragg flipped the card, examining it carefully under the light. "Interesting...a rare card and an auspicious one at that: *Grace.*

Gentlemen, we would have to play an official and complete Hand-of-Five, and we would have to check our hand against *The Book of Soule,* but it is safe to say *Grace* is one of the most sought-after faces in the game, and one of the most rare. I myself did not realize that the partial deck I keep and so seldom use contained it. Perhaps it is your presence here that has drawn it forth."

"What did we get on the hole?" I asked.

"Ah, the impatience of youth," the good doctor sighed. "As I explained, young man, we have no way of knowing without an official game, a full foursome of players who've sworn the oath, and *The Book* to consult, but it is fair to say, with *Grace* in hand, virtually any vexing Predicament or Potluck would be trumped."

"The single, modified hole we've played," the doctor continued, "is, I grant you, a woefully inadequate simulation of the deeper, more mystical powers of Soule. Yet still it managed to tease out an essential difference between the two of you. It gave me insight into the way you think, which will prove useful for our playing lesson."

"I thank you, gentleman, and as a token, I bid you take as a souvenir the mettle card I earlier dealt each of you, and a handful of the other cards, as many as you may require. The sooner the Island is rid of them the better. And it is fitting that the descendants of Caspar Johannes should be heir to his magnificent illustrations."

At the doctor's urging, Dad and I helped ourselves, putting a handful of cards in our pockets for safekeeping, and to show off to Mom when we got back home. To take the whole deck would have seemed immodest to Dad, I thought. So while I stuffed my pockets more eagerly than he did, I erred on the side of modesty in hopes of pleasing him—like the Scots who leave a drop of whiskey at the bottom of their cup and call it the angel's share.

As the first beams of sunlight in days landed prismatically on the cottage's windows, the two of us followed the legendary Harlan Cragg down the stone path to the first tee of the Evalon links. The doctor explained we would be dividing our nine holes into the sacred and numerologically significant Law of Thirds. For the first three holes, Dad and I would play our own ball as the doctor looked on, so that he might observe how we tackled the course individually, and without his guidance. The next three holes would comprise our playing lesson, wherein he would, he warned us, consider each and every shot a "teaching moment."

The final third of our round on the Links of Evalon would commence after we had holed out on number 6 green, at which point Cragg promised he would leave us. Dad and I would, he insisted, play the final three holes as a team in best ball format to test the very lessons we had learned, unhindered by the presence of our teacher. At all costs, he said, we must finish our round.

CALAMITY

Thirteen

On the tee beside us, Harlan Cragg sniffed the air, his legs spread wide as if to brace himself against some unseen force. The fog, it was true, had begun to lift sufficient to allow us a glimpse of the first, a slight dogleg right angling uphill toward the lodge.

"In the tradition of Soule, we will begin with a benediction to the course itself," the doctor said after a prolonged silence. "In this case, and in my humble opinion, the finest nine holes of links golf in the world. And," he added, with a hint of smile, "never a wait for a tee time."

"It's beautiful," Dad said. "A treasure."

"Theunis Grum designed it, though that's a well-kept secret."

"Willem Grum's father?"

"Yes, and a brilliant architect, as you shall soon see, though, curiously, he abandoned the course…orphaned it really…just a few years after finishing the green on the ninth. A dispute with the owners at the time provoked Theunis's ire, leading to his final and absolute renunciation of his creation. It seems they were willing to give up enough acres of their failed orchards for nine holes, but not, as Theunis was lead to believe, a second nine, which would have been laid out on the far side of the lodge, near where Ms. McIntosh's practice tee now stands. I suppose to a proud young architect newly arrived in America and bristling with ego, a nine-hole course seemed only half whole. But for me its very charm exists in its modesty. It is, by my reckoning, the finest layout on the planet."

"Why, Doctor?" Dad asked.

"Have you ever gone to a public beach, gentlemen, and watched as the beachcombers separate themselves into groups, each according to his or her truest self? Some stand at the edge, looking down from what seems a satisfying distance at the breath-taking scene before them. Others bunker down in the dunes, near enough to the sea to feel its power and breeze, near enough to have their feet sunk in the sand, but at a safe, romantic distance. And then we have the third group, the group that runs right up to the foot of the beast, plunging in, getting their feet wet. Who do you typically find in that group?"

"Lovers," Dad answered.

"And?"

"Children."

"And what do those two groups...lovers and children...have in common, would you say?"

Dad crossed his right leg over his left, leaning on his driver, as golfers do when they're waiting or otherwise absorbed in thought. "Both groups are truly alive."

"What do you mean by *alive?*"

"They're uninhibited ... free. Vulnerable."

"Vulnerable? My heavens, vulnerable to what?"

"To pain," Dad said. "To disappointment. To rejection ... And to pleasure."

"Precisely!" the doctor exclaimed, so loudly I jumped. "And that, to answer your question, is why links golf is the only true golf. It coos to our hero-golfer. It punishes him. It changes inexcusably and without warning. It seduces, and sometimes, very rarely, it grants him love unconditional and peace everlasting. And now, gentlemen, if you'll humor an old man, one more story as we wait for the fog to lift fully and for the flag to come into view."

Hearing no opposition, Cragg continued. "In my earliest days at Evalon, I and my staff used to wheel the badly disabled veterans down to the water's edge, assuming the air would do them good. We were shocked to learn, however, that the sound of the surf, the very crash and roar and explosiveness of it, conjured in many excruciating memories of the trenches. They said the waves when they crescendoed made the sound of a bomb cratering the earth. More precisely, they claimed the surf sounded, in its strength, force, and periodicity, like waves of bombers strafing an open field. Most refused to come back. Others agreed to return to the sea only after hours of therapy to rid them of their dreadful association and replace it with something less traumatic."

"My story relates to the superiority of the Links of Evalon inasmuch as a course, to be truly excellent, must have a skeleton in the closet… It must have a back door where the imp gets in. It must have an attic or a widow's walk where even the heroic fear to tread. For that is what draws lovers and children both. That's what makes it beautiful, and dreadful, all at once. And that, Robert and Jack, is what makes a layout like Evalon wonderful and terrible as a dream, a dream to which the golfer willingly succumbs even as he struggles to awaken."

Cragg swung himself around to face the ocean. "The sea wants in, gentlemen... It always has, and it always will. If it had its way, it would overrun our little island. It is, even now, chipping away at it, eroding it, seeing where it will give and where it will stand fast. The golfer, if he is brave, likewise seeks holes in himself, testing his mettle, shoring up or giving in. Here on Evalon and a few places like it, the battle is always on, always epic. Land combats sea. Golfer battles self. Links thwart golfer. And up on the hill, in the not-so-distant past, Evalon's insane wrestled with their very own demons. It's all of a beautiful, dramatic piece. That's why I live in my humble cottage behind the jetty, so I'm near enough to hear the sea's battle cries, which remind me that I am alive. And that, to your question, Robert, is why the Links of Evalon are the best in this or any other land."

After that kind of ode, it was difficult even to take a divot in what Cragg called a masterpiece of design and nature. But we did, and the doctor, who must have exhausted himself in praise, followed on our heels those first three holes not saying a word, walking briskly for a man of his immeasurable age. Several times, Dad and I attempted to engage him in conversation, but all he would say was, *Silence please, gentlemen.*

The first three holes at Evalon move inland—a par 4, a par 5 over a deep ravine, and a sharp dogleg left par 4, which I played with the advice from Augustus's Legacy Room ringing in my ears: *Don't cut doglegs unless you're prepared to be bitten.* Dad finished the stretch one over par, playing his usual steady, unperturbed golf and taking advantage of the fair weather that had becalmed the Island. I, on the other hand, wilted under the doctor's scrutiny, suffering three self-conscious bogeys en route to the fourth.

The fourth hole stretched out along the ocean, and it was here that the old pro clamped down on us like a bulldog. Though we had been expecting it, his advance came so swiftly and so forcefully, it was as if a wind had freshened on the ocean and blown ashore as a gale. He chastised Dad mercilessly for taking an iron on the short, driveable par 4.

"But Doctor, a driver will do me very little good here. It will leave me with an awkward pitch at best, or without recourse in one of the greenside traps."

"I don't care if it leaves you in more sand than Lawrence of Arabia. What's more artistic, Robert, a safe 5-iron to the middle of the fairway followed by another up to the green, or a driver smoked and pickled with herring right down the middle?" Spittle flew from the doctor's mouth as he barked out his rhetoric.

"That's not a very realistic outcome, Doctor."

Harlan Cragg looked like he had been socked in the gut. *"Realistic?* Wasn't it you back at my cottage who told me your intention was aesthetics, artistry? I ask you, did Van Gogh speak of the realistic?"

"I told you that my intention was peace. There's not much peace in a slashed and burned driver."

"Ah, but there's adventure in it. Jesus Christ, Robert. You'll have everlasting peace in heaven. This is earth. Humor an old man and hit the Big Dog."

I was secretly happy Harlan Cragg had won the battle of wills. What son doesn't want to see his father, a man of sense and discretion, cut loose? I had never known my old man to doubt his club selection, or to fuss much over strategy. He would dance his dance regardless. He seldom tried for a play beyond his imagining, figuring he would hit the best shot he knew he had in him.

At last Dad relented, whether to let go of decades of controlled play or to appease the old shrink, I'll never know. He swung out of his shoes, his usually classical move transformed into a powerful piston, his right shoulder finishing so high he had to raise his chin to make room. The ball soared straight and true, splitting the bunkers that guarded the green and rolling within a few steps of the dance floor.

"How did it feel, Robert?" Cragg asked, his arms folded in front of his chest.

"Forced," Dad said between clenched teeth, adding, as he let out a long breath, "but liberating."

Next, Cragg turned his savage attentions on yours truly. I had pulled a driver, and he crowded me as if we were player and caddy trying not to be overheard by a television crew. When he spoke,

I thought it must be some cruel joke, given the conversation he had had, moments ago, with Dad.

"What's the point of taking a driver here, son? You can't get home."

"I hit my woods as well as my irons," I insisted.

"Do you, now? I'm afraid the physics of golf clubs would beg to differ. A clubhead fractionally open or closed as you hit the wood will result in a miss exponentially greater than if you had hit the iron. Are you man enough to admit you are intimidated by your long irons?"

"I'm not intimidated by them," I grumbled. "I just don't like them."

"You don't like them because you find them difficult to hit. Is that it?"

I said nothing, not wanting to give the curmudgeonly old shrink any more ammunition.

"The play here for a boy your age is a long iron. Now, will you accept the wisdom of an old man or will you continue the head-strong ways of youth?"

"Dad never tells me what club to hit," I groused at the doctor. This apparently infuriated him, because he stood in silence for a good thirty seconds, biting his bulldog's lip.

"That is because your father is afraid of you. You are a tyrant and he's afraid." Cragg eyed me curiously, awaiting my reaction.

"Now wait just a minute, Doctor," Dad interjected. But Harlan Cragg raised his hand for quiet, and he got it.

"What about it, Young Jack? How do you like it that your father has, up until this very moment, been afraid of you, a mere thirteen-year-old boy?"

"Dad's not afraid of me."

"No? Then why didn't he knock you flat as a pancake when

you punched him on the golf course? Your insolence merited it, to be sure."

"Because," I said slowly, my words catching up with my thoughts for once. "He's a gentleman."

"And if he must endure the responsibilities of gentlemanliness, what absolves you? What if this were your last round with him, or worse yet, what if this round at Evalon had never come to pass, and your last golfing moment together was that ignominious hole on which you struck your father. You would have regretted it for the rest of your life."

"The trouble with all men," the old pro continued, waxing philosophic, "is that they address their own mortality not with the sober stratagems required of them on the golf course, but with the desperate flailing of the duffer seeking unearned grace... So, will you play the iron, Jack, or will you not?"

"I will," I sighed, pulling a 3 from my bag and hitting a lackluster shot off the toe that barely cleared the gully, and left me another long iron to the pin.

"Satisfied?" I muttered, figuring the decrepit shrink couldn't hear me.

"Yes," he said. "Quite. For a single hole, you have been broken of your mulishness. The shot itself is irrelevant."

The shot itself is irrelevant. It was the single most ridiculous thing I'd ever heard on a golf course. Still I trudged after Dad and Cragg, determined, at the very least, to get a round of golf in.

To his delight and to mine, Dad birdied the fourth, flipping a wedge up onto the green, easy as you please, and sinking a downhill six-footer to the restrained applause of the doctor and a whoop from me. Dad tipped his cap to both of us. He was having fun.

I, on the other hand, slapped the ball around that eternal

links like a minor league hockey player, cursing under my breath. I holed out for a triple-bogey 7, part of me wondering if grandpa Caspar had come back to life and pulled from his Pantheon deck the god of triple bogeys.

Evalon's fifth hole is a par 3 along the water, the ocean running the length of the right-hand side, and plays to a tightly bunkered green in a grove of cypress. As we arrived at the tee, the wind freshened again and Harlan Cragg looked into the sky above the sea and declared that once the wind blew itself out, the fog would return. And then he did something more curious still. He laid his hand on my father's shoulder and said, "Robert, how about you play this one from the tips."

Father was not a back-tee man. He didn't believe in overstatement or understatement, but in the Goldilocks principle of "just right." He maintained that the back tees were either a shameless stroke to the amateur's ego on courses where there was, at best, ten or fifteen yards difference between them and the middles, or, on the other hand, a test of the golfer's integrity and self-awareness requiring the occasional golfer to decline the silliness of playing the hole from a professional distance. For Dad, the choice of tee was a consideration of modesty as much as honesty.

"I'd prefer not to, Harlan," he said, calling the doctor by his given name for the first time. Already, it felt like we had known the old coot a lifetime.

"As you wish, Robert, but it would please an old man greatly if you would try. You've got the game for it, even here at Evalon."

Dad stopped for a moment, resting his bag on the back tee and flipping a few blades of grass into the wind, only to have them blow back in his face. The champion tees at number five played nearly 200 yards, excluding the two-club wind. After some considering, Dad put the club back in the bag, appearing to give up on the idea of the pro tees entirely.

"What do you think your father should do, Jack?"

Again, the old doctor had me trapped, or as Dad used to say, he had me between a rock and a hard place. I answered from my gut, which seemed to be the kind of reply Harlan Cragg would appreciate.

"Play it from the tips, Dad."

The doctor nodded approvingly. "There isn't a son in the world who doesn't want his father to be a hero."

Reluctantly, Dad hit that shot from the tips, hit it into a gust that by the time he and Harlan were through discussing it, had practically blown him over.

The shot was pure, the type that on an ordinary day back home would have been an all-timer, but on Evalon did well to claw its way to the fringe, giving my old man a legitimate shot at par on what was, without a doubt, the toughest par three either of us had ever faced.

My own shot from the regulation tees, was, at 140 yards, no less difficult for me. I pulled a 4-iron, figuring a two-club wind, and planned to hit it with everything I had. The doctor disagreed vehemently, which, I was coming to understand, was his habitual mode. He declared that if I swung hard the ball would only balloon into the wind, and I would lose the benefit of my strategy entirely. Why not take a 3-iron, he suggested, play it off my right foot, and swing easy, keeping the ball underneath the breeze.

On this one, the doctor proved right as rain, and I executed. The result was a green in regulation and pats on the back from both Dad and the doctor, as we walked together to the putting surface, reliving both of our shots in fine detail.

Dad and I both made pars on number five, leaving him at an unbelievable even par and me at a none-too-shabby six over.

Number six was a gargantuan Par 5, a dogleg right that played downhill from the tee into a valley, then uphill, blind, on a second shot to a green positioned on an epic swell of cliff. Again, the ocean menaced the right side, cutting in at the landing area atop the hill, in front of the green. It was to be the doctor's last hole with us.

"Gentlemen, into this wind neither of you will be reach, so put that misguided notion out of your feeble brains. But the question is not what concession speech you will deliver, because par here represents victory. The question before you now is what is the proper play from the tee, and that is the only question. Robert, it is your honor, play away please."

I noticed that the doctor used the word *play* frequently. One did not hit a golf ball, one *played* the golf ball. One did not plan a shot, he made a *play*. One did not have honors, he *played* away. As we stood there on the sixth tee, sheltered by a small clump of live oaks, I wondered if Dad noticed the same. As a consequence of the doctor's intimidating presence, we'd hardly spoken a word. It was as if Cragg was purposefully walking between us, separating us each into our own worlds.

Dad pulled a 2-iron and, without comment from the doctor or so much as a glance in the old curmudgeon's direction, striped it down the fairway at an impressive distance. When it came my turn I found myself paralyzed by doubt. Ordinarily, I would have hit a driver without a second thought, but the doctor's voice persisted, and I couldn't help but think back to our conversation on number 4.

Should I follow Dad's example and hit a long iron? Should I hit something less, maybe a 5-iron, and plan on four, straightforward shots for me to reach? Or should I take the Big Dog and try to roll it up alongside Dad's ball on the fairway? Involuntarily, I stole a glance at the doctor glowering from the back of the tee. "What are you looking at?" he groused. "Quickly, Jack, the fog will be back soon."

And so for reasons I only half understood, I did something I'd never done before and have never done since. Maybe the doctor's admonitions had so thoroughly addled me I had become a stranger even to my own golfing self. Or maybe the psychic intensity I felt emanating from him was so great I merely surrendered to it. Or maybe I was finally *playing* the game, knowing that there would be many hundreds of rounds left for me, and that I needn't fear modesty.

I pulled a 5-iron, put it back in my stance, and did little more than chip it down the fairway. The shot took off true and with surprising distance for an effortless swing, and landed just onto the fairway at distance of 150 yards—easily 175 or better minus the wind.

Cragg said nothing until we came to my shot in the fairway. Having played it safe from the tee, I left myself on the horns of another dilemma. To reach the lay-up area now would take the best 3-wood of my life, while a shorter lay-up at the base of the massive head of land on which the green perched required nothing more than another 5-iron.

I could feel the doctor's fierce gaze on me as I pulled first a wood, taking a few practice strokes, and then the 5 again which, when I gripped it, felt right. I looked at Cragg for confirmation, but he was already looking ahead, his hawkish profile turned toward me, his unkempt silver hair blowing wild in the wind.

I took the same swing as before, and the results proved as satisfactory as they had from the tee. It was the first time I had truly played one shot at a time, for by playing a club with which I was utterly comfortable and which left me without a prayer of reaching the green in the regulation three shots, I had put the thought of par out of my mind. I was playing, literally, within myself.

By contrast, Dad seemed to be playing out of his mind. He seemed almost a different man out there in the wind and wild, and I could feel the energy, the pure joy, illuminating him. I had no desire to speak to him but only to be near him, to revel in his presence.

The doctor, though, was still making house calls.

Dad had a 5-iron in hand for his second on the par 5, the same number I had played for my lay-up from farther back, only Dad's shot, aimed for the top of the hill, would be played for position.

Standing between Dad and the sea like a gaunt old tree, the doctor interjected, "A 5-iron is a sensible play; it will get the job done, but I think you've a better, braver shot in you."

Dad looked up from his practice swing, annoyed. Even he, in whatever transcendent state he was in, could not have missed the doctor's use of his—Dad's—very own phrase.

"That's the logic that got me in trouble when I played best shot with Jack, Doctor."

"That's the fascinating thing about golf, and life, isn't it, Robert?" The doctor had almost to shout to be heard above the surf. "They're both situational. Not like ethics, which is a world you know well, but more like weather. You would not wear a parka when a bathing suit was in order."

"Which is exactly why I intend to play a mid-iron, Harlan. Minus the wind and the wet, I might indeed be tempted to hit a wood up the fairway as far as I could, but in selecting an iron, I am adjusting my sails."

"An interesting metaphor, the sail." Cragg paused to consider. "You feel the wind pushing on you, and you surmise your power to control the ball has lessened. You attempt to play within yourself, is that the gist of it?"

"Right," Dad hollered back, the wind blowing bits of sand in our face so forcefully they felt like ice.

"What if I hold that the wind is not lessening your control any more than the sun would be, or the rain, or any other meteorological condition. The wind, in itself, is innocent of motivation. It is as natural as this turf," he said, kicking the bright green fescue beneath his toe, "or that sea hawk," he said, pointing to a raptor riding the thermals. "Trust me, Robert, the wind is calling forth your better shot. Remember, the ball fits. There's plenty of room on top of the hill to receive your play. I suggest you hit the kind of shot Young Jack here will one day feel compelled to tell his own son about. Hit the goddamned driver."

"Off the deck?" Dad asked, incredulous.

"Off the deck," Cragg said, unblinking.

As Dad looked down at his lie, a change seemed to come over him, a different cast of light.

"Why not?" he said finally, backing off the shot to pull the driver and realign himself. He grapevined up to the ball, waggling his clubhead en route with perfect concentration. He approached with the easy rhythm of a waltz, and I knew the shot would be a good one.

This one proved still more masterful than his tee shot on number four. The ball cut through the wind as if it had its own intention—beyond the one Dad had dispatched it with. It cleared the crest of the giant hill with room to spare.

After I played yet another 5-iron, my third in as many shots, we spied the old man's ball up ahead in the fairway, 10 yards short of the par-5 green—the very green Cragg had said from the tee we dare not dream of reaching in two.

But before we could survey Dad's approach, I had to play my

fourth from 110 yards out, again, straight into that devil of a wind. Until now, I had played the 5 on each and every stroke because it had been the club calling more loudly than the rest, the one that seemed natural and right in my hands, regardless of distance. Now, as I stood in the fairway preparing to hit my fourth shot, it appeared once more to be the only logical choice. In the course of playing the same iron three times in a row, it had become friendly to me, like an old hammer perfectly suited to the task. The doctor asked me if I was sure choosing the same number for four consecutive tries was the proper play—that word again—and I answered him calmly that it was. Was I sure, he wondered aloud, that I hadn't fallen in love with the club?

I chose not to answer. Instead, my feet found their target line. Again, though I faced a full shot, in my mind it felt like little more than a chip.

My approach hit once on the apron, once on the dance floor itself, and caromed into the wind-bent flagstick before dropping into the cup. It was the first time I had ever holed out from the fairway. Even the old doctor and Dad whooped and hollered from their outpost on top of the hill. A birdie!

"Run up and grab your ball from of the hole, Jack" the old doctor said, clapping me on the back when I reached him and Dad. "It's liable to jump out. And besides, the way your old man is playing, he just might roll his ball in on top of yours."

I scurried up to pluck my pearl from the jar, and stepped aside to await Dad's shot. He played quickly, the old man did, and for a second I thought his pitch would indeed follow suit, but the slope of the green won out, leaving him a five-foot downhiller for bird. "Gently now, Robert," I heard the doctor coo behind him. Dad did as he was advised, tickling it into the cup for his second birdie of the round. We left the sixth green in high spirits, all of us having settled into the rhythm of the round and of one another's company.

We arrived at the seventh, a short little par 3 playing dramatically downhill to a tiny, postage stamp green. It was the kind of a hole that begged to be photographed, a little pitch-and-putt hard by the sea that was inviting and impossible all at once.

"Here is where I must leave you." The doctor's pronouncement startled Dad and me from our reverie. In the six holes Cragg had been at our side, he had become a natural fact of our existence, a force so omnipresent it was almost not present at all.

"We'd be honored if you would finish with us, Doctor," Dad said, bowing slightly.

"And I would be honored, too, Robert." He extended his hand in friendship first to Dad and then to me. "But in golf as in life, all good things must end. It is perhaps the most timely lesson I can leave you with."

"No," the Doctor repeated, as if to convince himself of his choice, "if you wish to honor me, you will finish the round. But you must make haste... The fog will be here soon." He pointed out to sea, where an eerie cloud bank had formed and, as we bid him final farewell, begun to drift toward us.

The old pro walked off the tee, striking off at a diagonal across the sixth, back toward his cottage in the distance. Dad and I watched him go, feeling something like sadness, if it's possible to feel sadness for someone you have known only for an afternoon.

TREE TROUBLE

Fourteen

In the doctor's wake, the wind blew with unprecedented force.

Dad stood on the seventh tee looking like a human version of the wind-warped cypresses dotting Theunis Grum's orphaned links. Pant legs whipping in the gale, the old man removed his hat, steadied himself, and aimed a 4-iron at the 110-yard hole. He hit a stinger low into the teeth of the breeze, and it chased through the green. He would have a touchy downhill chip left.

Predictably, I pulled my tee-ball left, away from the water, the zephyr smothering it instantly and pushing it into the ice plant on the steep, ocean-facing slope. My second shot would be no less difficult than my first.

As we approached the green, the breeze died down without warning, as if the gods of golf themselves had becalmed it. And as I set up to lob my ball out of the spinach and onto that impossibly small dance floor, I saw the thick sea mist settle in as if, like an unwanted houseguest, it meant to stay for days.

For an instant, I completely lost sight of Dad behind the green. Fear seized me just as it had on the Janus Hole. Then the mist, so unreal it looked as if it had come from a Hollywood movie, passed, and again I could see his figure through the vapors. Still, I strained to make out the shape of him chipping the ball past the cup by some fifteen paces.

I almost stepped on my ball when I reached it where it had come to rest on the fringe, so walled in by fog had we become. Still, I was able to putt—in fact, I was able to putt it three times— for a double bogey. Dad, meanwhile, narrowly missed his comebacker up the hill and carded a bog. Still, he was even par for the round on a course that was tougher than any U.S. Open track, even Pebble.

The eighth tee, which jutted out on a small promontory immediately behind the seventh green, made for a blind tee shot, in more ways than one. Harlan Cragg had left us with no scorecard, no course map, no nothing. The yardages he had supplied before leaving us had come completely from his encyclopedic memory.

The old shrink's silence the last few holes lingered, and Dad and I barely spoke as we teed up on number eight. The only real topic of conversation would have been whether we should quit, as common sense said we should. But we both knew we couldn't, and wouldn't, so there was little else to do amid the ocean's roar than play the ball in the direction the tee pointed us, and hit the best shot we had in us. Dad chose an iron, I expect because his intuition told him the ocean would cut back into the hole at some indeterminate distance, and he did not want to feed the ungrateful sea an otherwise well-struck tee-ball.

I took an iron at first, then, recalling the doctor's advice to Dad about the wind on the sixth hole, decided that to dink it into the fairway because it would be easier to find in the fog would be a coward's move. So I played, or attempted to play, the best shot I had in me: a driver.

We didn't have a prayer of finding our shots leaving the tee. The only clue we had to their whereabouts was our private knowledge of our swing and our golf ball, just as we had imperfectly practiced with Ava McIntosh the day before. She had said that the dream of the shot was the shot. So, at this moment, with our pearls and our cause both appearing lost, it seemed the only thing we could do was add up all the similar shot-dreams we had ever had, average them down the middle, and make our best guess at our tee balls' final resting places.

Dad drifted right as we walked, to where he believed his well-hit long iron had come to rest, if indeed he could trust the lay of the land beneath him. I, on the other hand, headed left, where I supposed my clawing drive had skittered.

I set my watch for exactly five minutes, as Dad had taught me to do in the event of a lost ball, knowing that if I didn't find my wayward shot before the watch struck 5, I'd turn into a pumpkin, and have to declare it lost.

Returning to square one was not a realistic option. Even if I could find the teeing ground again without stepping off a cliff and plummeting into the ocean, I faced the same impossible, fogged-in conditions playing a provisional. As quickly as darkness was descending, I didn't have the luxury of stroke and distance. The choice was simple: find the ball, or end the round.

I looked for my pearl with mounting desperation, feeling the seconds tick by. I called out for Dad's help, but heard nothing, my voice lost in the wind and choked by the fog.

Four minutes and thirty seconds into my search, something caught my eye at the foot of a large cypress tree. A Soule card! Had one of the cards I pocketed at the cottage somehow been blown here on the breeze? What other explanation could there be? My mind raced through the possibilities, landing on one that, in its impossibility, was neither more nor less likely. Maybe Harlan Cragg had placed the card here on his way back. But he himself had said he was through with Soule. And, anyway, the chances of him leaving a card, and a Providence card at that, exactly where I would stumble onto it, fog-addled, seemed too remote to consider.

The Providence before me showed a boy not much younger

than me bending over a ball bathed in god-light. *Found,* the card read.

I looked from the card in my hand back to the place where I had chanced upon it, and there, unbelievably, laid my ball. I looked at my watch. Four minutes and fifty-eight seconds had elapsed. Maybe the card had been a treasure map marking the spot. Or perhaps the card hadn't been a finding aid at all but an attempt, by some trickster god, at a cover-up.

In any case, a game of Soule, the prototype version that Caspar and Willem had played on this very hole, had been commenced by the laying down of that card by an unknown hand. I had now to finish two games—life and golf—or were they one, as Caspar had maintained even in his madness.

I pulled what cards I had from my back pocket—the ones I had taken from the three decks the doctor had assembled for our modified hand back at the cottage. The Providence card having already been laid down for me, I had only to draw my own Pantheon and Predicament.

I spread the cards out quickly on the mist-dampened ground, seeing before me a whole new Elysian Fields of golfing gods and goddesses. Among them, I settled on *Cut Shot,* for that is what I would have to play to work my ball around the trunk of the tree and bend it back to the green. The Predicament card I knew I must draw blindly, and the draw proved prophetic: *Tree Trouble.*

No kidding.

I played the cut with a choked down 4-iron, having no idea the distance remaining to the green, the direction of the green, or anything, really, beyond the dream of the hole itself, as Ava had taught me.

Afterwards, I called out to Dad until my voice grew hoarse, the fog so thick I could barely see my shoes. I listened for the sea, knowing that it had been to our right off the tee. The sound seemed now to be coming from everywhere. I looked for the cypress from which I had made my last play, but it too had dissolved in the mist. I could not take more than a few tentative steps in any direction for fear of either stepping off a shear edge into the sea, or unknowingly walking away from the green rather than toward it.

At last I sat down in the middle of the fairway—right on the stack of Soule cards buried in my back pocket. The first card I fingered read *Clear Path.* Its providence showed a gap not wider than a hallway in a wall of trees, and in the distance, like a small luminous lighthouse, a flagstick.

The card behind it was a Predicament announcing *Confusion,* and showed a golfer raising two clubs at once, brow furrowed. An angel fluttered near the top of one club while a devil menaced the other.

A third face, completing the trinity in the modified game the doctor had taught us, fell out of my stack—a Pantheon introducing *Straight Shooter,* a serious deity holding a 1-iron stern as a pitchfork. Behind him, a perfectly geometric series of corn rows converged at the horizon.

The cards had played themselves. And when I looked up from my irregular Hand-of-Three, I saw that indeed the Providence and Pantheon card had already mingled to make my fate. Before me lay a clear path to the green, as if the curtain of fog itself had been parted. And at the end of that long column lay a golf ball... my golf ball!

I scrambled to my feet and ran for it, my clubs rattling at my shoulder. When I arrived I found the ball had barely trickled onto the putting surface, and, since I did not have the Soule deck that governed putting, there would be no new cards to lay down until my tee shot on number nine.

I was on my own with the flat stick. I stroked the ball quickly, afraid of losing the divine sightline the cards had bestowed. It took me two to get in—a par. Overjoyed, I sprinted to the final tee. As I did, the path provided by the Providence card demateri- alized, leaving me once more in an impenetrable fog.

I lingered on the ninth, wondering what my next move should be. I could wait here for Dad, but what if he had already played through? It had taken me a long while to play the eighth and, if he had even marginally better luck than I had, he would be well down the ninth by now. I could, I figured, locate the rough-line where the fairway met the taller grass and, by taking baby steps, follow it home to the ninth green.

But I had promised to finish the round, and so had the old man. We were, after all, playing a best ball for the last three holes, and there was no telling what score Dad had recorded on the eighth. We might need my par there. Had Dad's hot streak ended, I reasoned, our team might even use whatever score I could mus- ter on the ninth. Again I had no idea of the shape of the hole, or of the shot required, but only that I must play it, by the cards and by the clubs.

The first draw from the deck this time was a Pantheon. It read simply *Water Hazard* and showed Neptune riding a roiling sea holding a golf club in place of a trident, the tide below him grasp- ing and grabbling in the shape of a thousand hungry hands.

The next card out of the deck proved to be a Predicament, and this too spelled trouble—*Water's Edge,* it read, showing a bird's- eye view of a golfer's feet in address position, his ball on the edge of a cliff and, far below, a harrowing ocean. The first two cards from the deck had a daunting effect on me. I began to understand how Willy Grum must have felt on the day the cards foretold he would be struck half blind.

I blinked when I drew my third and final providential card—
Grace once more...the very same I had drawn in the doctor's cottage, the one he had claimed was incredibly rare. Had I inadver-
tently put that same card back in my pocket? I was sure I hadn't,
as the doctor had expressly directed us to take our souvenir cards
from the pile unplayed.

Had the doctor lied? Had he stacked the deck? Did he realize
in advance that a fog-inspired game of Soule, a game of chance,
faith, and fate, would finally be required of me on the Links of
Evalon? I had a feeling he had. And if he had, to have his students
leave his cottage with a small number of cards safely stowed away
in their back pockets in case of emergency would be as life-saving
as aces up their sleeves.

Grace—showing an enormous god-hand offering   the
redemption of a golf ball retrieved from a watery grave—stared
back at me. Holding the card, I appreciated Caspar's genius more
than ever. What could be more emblematic of grace than a ball
mysteriously returned from the deep?

I pulled out a driver, dreaming the unseen hole before me as
a sturdy par 4 to culminate Evalon's stern test of seaside links. I
swung not knowing what the unlikely mix of cards would bring,
nor what the intention of my swing would add to the mix. The
drive was strong but pushed terribly out to what was surely, and
sadly, the sea.

Just off the tee, my feet found cliff's edge. Beneath me, the
surf battered the rocks with a force that seemed to shake the
Island. I followed the cliff edge carefully at a distance of maybe a
few feet, counting off my paces as I went in an attempt to estimate
yardage.

I found my ball on the 219th step—not more than six inches from the ravine that tumbled to the sea—*Water's Edge* just as the cards had predicted. Its coming to rest here could be nothing short of an act of grace. My push from the tee had been more like a shank.

I played my next three cards, or rather they played me. The god governing the shot was revealed to be *Wind-cheater,* the Predicament was the ever-present *Fog,* and the Providence was *Homecoming,* a card showing, in the foreground, a young man wearing a college sweater hugging his parents and, in the background, his jalopy pulled up in the drive, golf clubs and dirty laundry spilling out.

I swung with a deeper sense of trust than I had ever known, though I could scarcely see my ball. And though one slip might indeed have sacrificed me to Neptune, I swung with a sense of purpose and beauty, a swing Dad would have been proud to see. The ball took flight in a positive direction, at the expected trajectory. I chased after it into a soup of fog, using the sheer coastline as the road home.

When the grass at cliff's edge turned suddenly close cropped, I looked left for the ninth green, and there a ball gleamed like manna in the mist, having come to rest a mere 12 feet from the jar. I sat my bag down on the fringe, smiling as I pulled my putter out to survey the line—a delicate left-to-right breaker.

When I bent to wipe the mud from its dimples, I discovered another surprise straight from the gods of golf... It wasn't my ball at all.

"I wouldn't putt that if I were you. Unless you want a two-stroke penalty." The voice, familiar as my own, came from the side of the green. There, sitting on the short grass, his long legs stretched out in front of him, was Dad.

I ran and hugged him around the neck. "Careful," he said,

"don't muss me. That putt's for birdie!" He shooed me away playfully. "Your ball's back there, kiddo," he said, pointing over his shoulder to the thick rough behind and left of the green. "You damn near brained me with your approach."

I was so relieved to have found him, and to have found the home hole, I played my wedge before I thought to draw my Hand-of-Three from the Soule deck. Oblivious to the cards, I opened the clubface and flopped it to within 15 feet. The Soule draw, when, after the fact, I remembered to make it, was in agreement. Still, my fate wouldn't figure in our score if Dad sunk his twelve-footer.

The old man took an unusual amount of time over the putt for birdie on the last at Evalon, seeming to savor it. Readied, he stroked it smoothly, the ball trundling toward the hole, and, on its final revolution, tumbling into the cup for a three. He tipped his cap to me, smiled, and bent down to remove the ball, lithe as Sammy Snead.

"Go, on, Jack," he said, throwing his ball up into the air and catching it smartly. "You promised the doc you'd finish, and finishing means holing out." He pointed to the fifteen feet of work I had left to do with the flat stick.

For the record, I missed the par, but I didn't much care. I had lost myself but found my partner. And as I walked off the ninth arm and arm with him, I considered it nothing short of an act of grace.

FRIENDSHIP

Fifteen

By the time Dad and I walked across the Island to the lodge, peeled off our drenched clothes, and warmed ourselves by the fire, it was nearly 8:00 clock. We ordered room service to celebrate what had been an incredible day—conquering the Janus Hole, meeting the legendary Harlan Cragg, playing our first modified game of Soule, enduring the doctor's in-your-face playing lesson, and finally finding our way through an impenetrable fog, by the clubs and by the cards, to finish our first ever round together.

We had knocked on the door of the doctor's cabin after holing out on the ninth. We had knocked many times, in fact, calling out his name above the roar of the ocean. We had seen light leaking from beneath his shutters, but we had dared not rap on the windows themselves, for fear of the doctor's wrath.

I had felt something like love for the gruff old shrink on the fifth hole, and something like abandonment when he'd left us on the seventh. And standing in the dusk outside his cottage, soaking wet and cold, I had felt something like disgust. Never, except perhaps with Dad, had I felt such conflicting emotions about one person.

Dad had said not to give the doctor's disappearance a second thought. It was just his way. Cragg might have walked straight from the seventh tee where he left us to the lodge, Dad told me, as the routing of the course had brought him closer to the imposing hotel than he would otherwise have been. Maybe he hadn't been home when we'd knocked after all.

Dad had shared the rest of his round with me on the way back to the hotel. He, too, had feared his tee shot lost on the eighth when, just as I had, he'd stumbled upon a Soule card illustrating his predicament. *On the Rocks,* his draw had read. And, just as I had, he had played what cards he had in his pocket, and, sure enough, the ball had revealed itself, up against a rock, as foretold.

Recollecting Willy Grum's long-ago, eyes-bigger-than-his-stomach foolhardiness, the old man had played out sideways back into the fairway, a mere chip of some 15 yards that he'd been able to locate—barely—so thick was the fog. He'd then drawn his next hand, playing a short iron onto the green and two-putting for a bogey, dropping him back to one over par.

He'd waited for me on number 9 for what must have been ten minutes, he said, before he'd realized the best thing he could do would be to wait for me on the green…if he could find it. He'd worried for me, too, he told me, but he knew, as he put it, that he hadn't raised a fool. If the fates willed it, as he suspected they would, we would meet up again on the home hole.

We'd walked almost all the way back to the lodge when Dad, interrupting his story, had turned to me, gravely, and said, "Jackie, I played all my cards."

"That means you're done with your game of Soule," I'd told him. "You win!"

"A modified game, anyway. Imagine, Jackie, playing with 50 of those cards and a separate deck for putting, and having to draw to replace your discards. I only took four from Dr. Cragg's deck, and, as it turned out, I needed every last one of them."

"I probably took a dozen," I'd admitted.

Dad had looked down at the ground then. "The trouble is, son, I accidentally turned over my…mettle card."

"What was it?"

"It was remarkable," he'd said, lost in thought.

We'd walked into the lodge, got cleaned up, and sat down to tally our better-ball score beside the roaring fire in our Dark Horse room—the world's greatest golfing underdogs watching from the walls.

Our team net turned out to be a one-under-par 35 on the Links of Evalon, best ball, for which we had used my score on just one of the holes, the eighth. Even with his bogey on that same, fateful hole, Dad had shot a remarkable 36, even par. He held the scorecard right up in front of his nose, as if he didn't believe his eyes. He pledged we would frame it when we got home. He said he had played the very best golf he had in him.

I couldn't quite say the same for myself, but I had, realized, played with a deeper sense of feeling, of higher purpose, than ever before, and I had, as a 13-year-old kid, held my own on a lengthy, seaside course in the worst possible conditions. I had done something, Dad claimed, no other golfer my age could have done, and he assured me that the kind of pluck I had shown on the Links of Evalon would have translated into a par round on any normal course. I had a feeling he was right, and yet I knew that golf must never be a game of "would haves."

After we had basked sufficiently in the glow of our round, Dad asked me if I would run downstairs and call on Augustus. He said he wanted the librarian's opinion on his mettle card. Would I ask him to meet us in the library in fifteen minutes, and would I wait for the archivist to make sure he got there?

So, for the second night in a row, I darkened Auggie's door, rousing him from whatever smoke-filled pipedream he had embarked on. He answered, as before, in his smoking jacket and slippers. And when I gave him the Reader's Digest version of what had happened to Dad and me, his eyes got wide as saucers and he said, yes of course, he'd be down straightaway.

That's how we found ourselves back in the library at that spooky hour, crowded once more around Augustus's cluttered desk. Auggie said he had not heard of the Janus Hole being played in years from the floating tee, and, further, that in all his years on the Island he had known only two players to shoot par or better on the Evalon links, Willem Grum and Dr. Harlan Cragg.

Auggie had just finished pouring a whiskey toast to Dad's round, when the library door squeaked open. "Who goes there?" he called out.

We heard the shuffling of feet and a cacophony of wheezing and throat-clearing and grunting. Our long-suffering librarian rolled his eyes and shouted, "Confound you! If I have told you once, I have told you a thousand times, the library is closed!"

The Soule foursome had returned.

"Christ," the librarian muttered. "Six years of university education to baby-sit a bunch of old fogies playing that wretched game. The irony slays me."

Dad, shutting the door gently on the foursome as they settled into their never-ending dealing, began to tell Augustus the details of our modified game of Soule and about the simultaneous playing of cards and golf to divine our way around the storied links.

He saved for last the detail of the mettle card, which he said he had a powerful urge to share with us that very night, our last on the Island. Our ferry ride back to the mainland had been scheduled for early the next morning.

The archivist listened intently to the recounting. When Dad finished, he said, "I am of two minds, Robert. The first being that I concur with Dr. Cragg, that any playing of Soule, however modified, is likely to have a residual effect on one's fate, so powerful are the cards. If anyone would know, it would be the doctor. His living memory is deeper than anyone's on the Island."

"On the other hand," he continued, stroking his bushy mustache, "I would dearly love to see another mettle card, so that I might make an impression of it for our collections. The urge to view it is almost beyond my power to resist."

Dad paced the office, acting like he was ready to speak on several occasions, but ultimately staying mum. At last, he said. "Fellows, I am going to show you my hand. First, because my par round suggests the Soule card has already worked its magic. Second, because I am out of cards, having played my way down to the last, which, as Augustus explained yesterday, means in theory that I have completed my round. And if I have completed my round, I am entitled to turn over my Soule card and learn of my essential character, and, by extension, of my fate."

"Third, if I have already, and completely by accident, laid eyes on my mettle card, I ought to share its revelation with those close to me, which would be the natural course of things if I had, in fact, finished a Soule round of eighteen holes. One did not keep the truth of one's mettle card to one's self. Auggie, as you yourself explained, it was known throughout by the playing partners and by the Soule Master. Fourth and finally, I require assistance with its interpretation. That's where you come in, Augustus."

"You're using me for my Soule interpretation skills?"

"Precisely," Dad said, letting his smile give way to a thoughtful pause. "I would like Jackie to see it first."

I breathed deeply, feeling at once the weightiness of the moment, and the lightness of being Dad's chosen one, his right-hand man, his partner. Looking me in the eye, Dad handed me the card without fanfare.

When I was finished, he said, "And now your turn, Augustus..."

The librarian's eyes widened as they regarded Dad's card. He laid it down, face up, on the one small area of unoccupied desk space in front of him.

"Whatever you say to me, Augustus, I want you to say it to Jack, too. There will be no secrets between father and son."

"Robert," Augustus managed finally, "I would strongly recommend you talk with Dr. Cragg before you leave in the morning…"

"At 6 a.m., Augustus? I don't think so. And besides, if the doctor is as all-knowing as he appears, he already knows the hand he dealt me, and he's not answering his door. You're our best hope."

"Very well, then," the hard-pressed librarian sighed. "You should know that the card you hold is the most feared and the most sought-after among all the mettle cards, which are as many and as varied as the characters of golfers." Auggie cleared his throat. "Yours is the card *Peace Everlasting*. He turned the image toward us to point out its features. "Here you see a golfer in silhouette, hitting his ball into the last ray of twilight, a veritable afterglow. Around him, an angel choir emerges from the trees with heralding trumpets."

"What are they heralding, Augustus?"

"They're heralding a golfer's passage from this…from one world…one state of awareness and being, into the next. It is a supremely rapturous moment, a transcendent one."

"Then why are you having such difficulty talking about it?"

"Frankly, Robert, I am a bit overwhelmed at the sight of it here in my office, at this very moment. You must understand. I can say more at another time but…"

Just as Auggie labored to conclude his thought, I cry of startled joy rang out from one of the old men in the library.

Soooooooooooooule!

We rushed into the reading room to find that the playing of the last game of Soule on the Island, or anywhere in the world for that matter, had ground to a halt. The old man who had appeared all along to be the ringleader of the rogue band turned toward us, wide-eyed, putting his hands in the air as if he had just been arrested, but, more to the point, to show us that, beyond a shadow of a doubt, he had played his last card. The dude's playing partners agitated among themselves, making noises of disbelief and admiration and awe all at once.

Then the man who had cried *Soule* began to weep. While his playing partners looked on, magi-like, the old man cried and cried and cried until he could cry no more. He seemed at a point of great relief. He had, quite literally, completed the round of a lifetime. The race had not been to the swift.

When finally he ceased his blubbering, he looked up at us with hound dog eyes and said, in what was almost the voice of a child, "My mettle." Furtively, he reached for the one card left face down on the table, the card he had been carrying for countless years.

He clutched the card to his chest for a moment, sneaking a child's glance at it as we watched. And then he did what I suppose politeness would have required him to do but which was a grand and generous gesture all the same. He showed it first to his playing partners, who nodded, tears now streaming down their faces, too, then to Augustus, and finally to Dad and me, two complete strangers but, he must have sensed, kindred souls.

The card showed a foursome, their arms thrown over one another's shoulders, smiling big as if after their best-ever round. The mettle card read simply *Friendship*.

Though he could not find the words, the man thanked Augustus as best he could for allowing their game to continue. The archivist was demure, saying only a fool would have stopped such a long-standing tradition.

Augustus Repartee shot two photos that evening, two he insisted were necessary for posterity. The first was of the last foursome of Soule, at their happiest hour, arms around one another in a pose reminiscent of the mettle card. The other was a picture of Dad and me, likewise arm in arm, Dad holding his even-par scorecard aloft from that blessed afternoon on the Links of Evalon.

HOMECOMING

Sixteen

After ushering out the delirious, teary-eyed Soule players, Augustus asked me if I might run to his chambers and fetch his pipe. The evening's events had shaken his nerves, he said, and a little tobacco cure would do him well.

I obliged, looking everywhere for that blasted pipe until, after many minutes had passed, I gave up and returned to the library to find Augustus already smoking. He apologized profusely, saying he had discovered it on his desk a few moments after I left and had expected me to return straightaway, empty-handed.

In my absence, Dad and Auggie had been talking about weighty matters, I could tell. On my return they bade one another a hasty good night and good luck, the two men first shaking hands, then hugging. When they separated, both had a tear in their eye, and so did I, because I was sad to see Dad part from a new friend. He was particular about his companions, and like most people who are choosy, he didn't have very many.

I asked Dad on the way back to the Dark Horse room what he and Auggie had talked about. He said only that they had discussed life. He changed the subject, bringing the conversation back to the conclusion of the game of Soule we had just witnessed, talking endlessly about how fortunate we had been, what an epic journey that foursome had undertaken those many, many years. He said the old man's mettle card had been an apt one.

And did Dad think his own mettle had been an apt, I asked. He weighed his answer carefully. "Yes," he said, hugging me close.

The following morning Dad and I rolled out of bed to the alarm, quickly gathering up the few items left unpacked from the night before, and hastening to catch Charles's 6 a.m. ferry, the only "scheduled departure" for the mainland that day. Ava McIntosh, beautiful as ever, turned up to hug us on the mist-enveloped pier, the very image of an old black and white movie heroine waving her heartfelt bon voyage. Jacobsen, too, looking like he hadn't slept, showed up to clap us on the back for what he called the round of a lifetime. The doctor did not appear to bid us farewell. He had meant what he said: his sentiments would rest in the legacy of our playing lesson together on the Links of Evalon.

Not surprisingly, we were once again Blackbeard's only passengers. Dad asked why we couldn't leave at a more reasonable hour, to which Charles replied, "Orders of Dr. Cragg."

When we arrived back to the coast, Charles took our hands in his and said he hoped to see us again at Evalon. Something in his eyes told me he was trying to stick to the script Harlan Cragg had given him, and that had he not felt it a breach, he would have said more, much more. A ferryman is a ferryman because he sticks well to his route.

Grum was waiting for us in his wagon. We loaded our clubs in the back just as we had three days earlier. Dad surprised Grum and me both by announcing that his days at Evalon had made him unexpectedly homesick, and that he would like to be taken into town to book us the first flight home.

We shared nothing of what we had learned of the shepherd's past with Grum himself, our savant golfer turned half-blind chauffeur. Ours was a silence mutually observed. Grum, it seemed, had sent us to Evalon in part to share a personal story he could not find the words to tell. Now Dad and I were in the same predicament. We had experienced so much in our few days on the Island that no amount of telling would suffice.

The ride back proved the most pleasant hours I ever spent in the company of the two men. I laid on my back in the bed of the wagon, drifting in and out of sleep to the comforting sound of Dad and Grum speaking amiably to one another.

We stayed on the coast just two more days, Dad busily putting his things in order and me working hard on my golf game in the meadows above Grum's cabin.

I worked on my wall, too, which Grum had toiled on modestly in my absence. I did so with a newfound respect for the old man. And though I did mortar a few more foreign items into the wall, I did so less to antagonize him as to keep to my pattern. Including the bits and bobs of flotsam and jetsam washed up by the tide had become a matter of architectural integrity.

Sometimes, in the midst of placing a particularly difficult stone, I'd look back at the old man dozing/not dozing in the sporadic sun of those last couple of days, and think what a marvel it was that he was who he was, that I had come to know him, that he had befriended grandpa Caspar, that they had, in their own small way, made golfing history together, and that that history now included Dad and me.

When we left, it was Grum who carried us into town in his buggy, the kids even then pointing and laughing at the old man's outmoded method of transport. None of them had ever seen anything other than an automobile on their streets.

Grum was part of local lore because he dared to be. But more than that, he was a fixture in that sleepy seaside village every bit as much as Dr. Harlan Cragg was a fixture at Evalon Island. You could not have had one without the other.

We did not hug Grum before we climbed into the taxi waiting to take us to the airport; his peculiarly oval shape made him a difficult man to embrace. Instead, Dad set one hand on each of his broad shoulders, looked straight into those dim, unfocused eyes, and said he valued his friendship more than he would ever know, that he considered it a miracle that he had met Grum in the first place.

I swear, standing there, looking into Grum's wall-eye, that I saw a tear slip from it to the dusty gravel beneath his ponderous feet. But then again, it could have been the tear in my own eye.

As I turned to go, he said "C'mere, m' boy," and gave me a long, awkward, heartfelt squeeze. And then, as I pulled away, he said, "You'll always have a home at Grum's cabin."

Less than a week after we said our farewells to Grum, Dad was dead of an embolism. The coroner said the bubble may have formed on the long flight out to the coast, but that there was no way of knowing for sure.

I was thirteen when he passed, two young to be without him. Neighbors, strangers, law office clients, all of them came to tell Mom and me what a good and gentle man he had been. They said life just wasn't fair, and they were right.

A few months after Dad died, a letter arrived from the West Coast, addressed "Master Jack Johannes" and bearing the letterhead of the Evalon Golf Academy with Augustus Repartee scribbled by hand beneath. When I opened it, I found a folded piece of Evalon letterhead on which Augustus had written, in a beautiful hand, a note of condolence.

He explained that the night he had sent me to look for his pipe he had told my father that the mettle card he had drawn, in addition to promising peace everlasting, foretold the end of one's mortal life, and the beginning of the next. It was, Augustus had explained, the card of afterlives, though he had hastened to assure Dad that Soule was, after all, just a game, and that Dad had not taken the oath nor played a proper round.

Dad, Augustus wrote, had listened carefully and had expressed the desire, then and there, not to write an epitaph for the library's Legacy Room, but to write a letter addressed to me, his son. He was including it here, Augustus wrote, along with the photo taken our last night at Evalon, as he had promised Dad he would should the mettle card prove prophetic.

The librarian closed his letter by telling me that he considered me a son and that he hoped I would consider Evalon a second home.

I let Dad's letter to me sit on my dresser for days, unable to face it. I was furious at the gods who brought about such a fate, and I was overcome with grief and loss.

Shortly thereafter, after I had cried myself completely out of tears and lay on the floor wondering what would become of Mom and me, I snatched the letter down from the dresser, and began reading.

PEACE
EVERLASTING

Seventeen

Partner,

Things don't always turn out as we expect.

You will think at times that I have abandoned you, just as I thought of my father. Please don't think that. In this life, we are fortunate to have good partners for however long we have them. My round with you has, if you are reading this, been far too short. And yet you have taught me more about myself, and more about love, than I thought possible.

Understand, in case you should ever doubt, that you come from noble people. Understand that you should be a man of integrity, patience, and acceptance, and that you need never trifle. Understand that life has a plan for you, and that you have plan for it—that you and the gods work together on your fate, and that whatever you do and wherever you go, you bring your own power, your own light.

I could prattle on endlessly with advice, which, to you now, will only feel like salt in a wound. In the end, you and your mother were my dearest partners in everlasting peace, a peace that exists in having come to know you not just as a son, but as a young man. It may have taken us thirteen years to achieve our partnership, but the race isn't always to the swift, now is it?

Never forget the lessons we learned on the Links of Evalon. Never hit a club merely because it is familiar. Never sacrifice beauty for practicality or practicality for beauty, but insist on both. Play each round as if it were your last. Play the hand dealt you, not the one that you might have wished for.

I drew for my mettle card a golfer in a beautiful twilight, a twilight that came too soon and was full of angels. I wonder which card you drew that afternoon? But then, as your partner in this game of life, I already know.

If, in my absence, you should ever feel lonely, or out of place, or at odds with the world, remember what Grum always said to you about that wall of yours, "M' boy that stone seems to like it there."

Be that stone.

Savor your heritage, son, look after your mother, and remember that the dream of the shot is the shot.

Love always,

Dad

SALVATION

Eighteen

Drew and I wake to a thick fog after an intense day of storytelling. He's made me a birthday card, and stuck it to a loose wire on the fireplace screen in Grum's cabin. *Happy 6-0!,* it reads. *A good age and a better golf score!* The card's exclamation points and its big block lettering—a boy's hand, not a man's—make me smile.

After we've perked my coffee and cooked his oatmeal over the fire, we meander up to the Big House to poke around. After listening to my story of how his grandpa and I learned of the one-eyed shepherd, Drew wants to get a better look at Grum's 5-iron, the one Willy fashioned so long ago in the shop behind Harlan Cragg's cottage, the one that put his good golfing eye out. It's a relic, the only tangible evidence here or anywhere of the mystery that is the Links of Evalon.

Drew picks up the magic stick and waggles it, absorbing a little bit of the Willem Grum mojo. Now would be a perfect time, my son safely beside me, to dig more deeply into Grum's tomb for clues—old letters or champion's medals—anything that might further lift the veil on his life, and grandpa Caspar's. But it isn't our place. If anyone should be sifting through the layers of Grum's past, it's his son, Peter. Though I had only that one fated autumn with the old shepherd as he supervised the building of my wall, I feel so close to him I sometimes forget he has a real flesh and blood son, one who's got a dozen more years of gray hair atop his head than me.

Some stones are better left unturned.

"I can't believe he made this with his own hands," Drew says, setting up to an imaginary shot with the 5-iron, aligning himself by means of the old wooden floorboards. The Big House has been long since abandoned, Peter's occasional visits the only thing preventing it from yielding completely to the wind and the rain and the raccoons.

"Check out that sweet spot." I point to the dime-size area where impact after impact has worn a shiny bull's-eye in Grum's clubface. Golf clubs, like shoes, can be reverse engineered to reveal the habits of their owner. A man walks on his heels, the heels of his shoes become worn in a telltale pattern. A man hits it off the toe his whole life, his sweet spot moves slightly right of center. There's no arguing with the evidence. And the evidence says in his heyday Willy Grum never missed.

I take the club from Drew and waggle it a few times myself, the first time I've picked up a club in forever. My hands wrap easily around it, grateful to rehearse the sure grip they knew back when I was thirteen and staring down the eighth hole at the Links of Evalon.

I flip the clubhead up for closer inspection.

"Hate to be a party pooper, son, but they didn't start making this model until decades after Grum left the Island." I let the imposter club drop to the floor with a depressing thud. "Looks like our wily, one-eyed shepherd pulled the wool over our eyes."

"Maybe it's just a new clubhead," Drew says, doing his best to salvage the dream. "It's probably the original shaft and grip."

"I don't think so, champ." I hold the too-new shaft up to the light. "Anyway, it's still a special club. It's still Grum's."

"Ya," Drew mumbles.

We poke around a little while longer, both of us feeling the loneliness of the old house. Drew and I have grown used to being around people in our lives, unlike Grum and Dad, who could go weeks on end without seeing anyone but one another. Drew and I are different creatures from a different generation. But a part of me knows, too, that if we were to spend the same amount of time here that Dad and Grum once did, we'd likely fall right in line. That's the way the cards are dealt.

On the way out I remind Drew we should leave things as we found them, especially Grum's old rolltop desk. I wait for him at the door, calling in after him to hurry up.

"Dad, you better come in here."

Drew's standing at Grum's desk, stock still. He looks exactly as I did in the pictures snapped in this very room when I stood contemplating my own drawings or letters back home to Mom. I would never fully turn around for the camera—I was too cool—and as a result, the few photos Dad took of me at Grum's invariably featured me in profile.

I walk up behind Drew and lay my hands on his shoulders. He's holding a copy of Grum's old journal, *The Seeker*, open in his hands. Wordlessly, he points to the notices page.

Someone has taped the old advert for the Evalon Golf Academy, the one that sent Dad and me off on a dream so many moons ago, back in its original place. Written diagonally across it in permanent marker is the word *REDEEMED*.

"Why would Peter take the time to do that?" I wonder aloud.

"Probably 'cause of this," Drew says. With his free hand, he waves a small piece of paper at me about the size and shape and weight of a reply card.

"You sure you don't want to be sitting down for this?" my kid asks me.

"Nah. Hand it over."

What I read on the card leaves a golf ball-sized lump in my throat.

The Evalon Island Golf Academy
Announces the opening of its new season.
Ferries departing for a once-in-a-lifetime education.

It's an almost perfect carbon copy of the original invitation Dad and I received so long ago. And paper-clipped to it is a note from Willem Grum's only son.

> *Found this notice when I picked up the mail in town. Thought you two blokes might be interested. As we say in S'Africa, "Hop to!"*

After a long pause, Drew turns to me, all boy again, and asks, "Dad, can we go?"

∿∿∿

We pack in a mad rush. For the first time in days, the sun shines. Drew puts on his shades, and we close the door finally on Grum's cabin, not knowing when, or if, we'll be back. We set off diagonally across the back meadow toward the wall—my wall—that marks the lane and, beyond it, the gate where, in a few minutes, our taxi is due to arrive.

After days of solid gray, Drew and stumble down the path like two moles. The sunlight glints off the broken green glass shards and calico marbles and Cadillac-pink clamshells and plastic baby heads I long ago cemented into the wall to spite the shepherd.

I've never seen my wall—the work of a long-ago boyhood— in this light. It's twisted and surreal and absolutely beautiful. Amazing what art an old man and a young one can create when left to their own devices.

Drew walks in front of me, like he used to when he was younger, calling back over his shoulder every so often, "C'mon,

Dad."

I stop, for something at the very end of the wall, the last section completed, catches my eye. As I bend down to examine it, the golf clubs slung over my shoulder spill out onto the cobbled lane.

There, mortared in my wall, is a clubhead, rusted to a fine patina. A feeling, slow and steady as the first ray of sun, warms me from within. I move closer, reading the number on the face, a "5."

Engraved in the half-century-old, handmade clubface is a message from Grum, to me, and to eternity:

A one-eyed shepherd trumps a dim-witted boy.

⋏⋏⋏

"You sure you want me to drop you here?" our cabbie asks. I don't blame him. He's a good man, a Samaritan. He thinks I'm endangering myself and my son by asking him to let us off here in the boonies.

When he'd helped Drew and me load our clubs into the trunk, we'd told him we were going to a weekend golf academy off the coast. Then I'd advised him of our point of disembarkation—not a train station or an airport terminal or a bus depot, but a little inlet where once was an old ferry port.

"The *what* port?" he'd asked, confused.

"Never mind," I'd said. "I'll tell you when we get there."

Now, when I say, *Stop, this is the place*, he says, "Seriously?"

Drew and I pay our fare, sling our clubs and luggage over our shoulders, and plunge into the head-high reeds, laughing and shoving like brothers. Behind us, I hear the cabbie idling, no doubt hanging around to see if it's all a joke.

Zachary Michael Jack

Drew and I watch the sea from the same narrow stretch of rocky beach where, a generation ago, my old man and I waited for our ship to come in. The old dock is nowhere to be seen, long ago washed to sea. The Evalon pier once tucked in the reeds has gone missing, too. No moony honeymooners greet us. No signs announce the next ferries to depart.

"You sure about this?" Drew's voice, uncertain, comes from behind me. "Want me to see if the cab is still here?"

I look at my phone...no reception. No way back to town. No goddamned luck. I don't know how to answer him.

"You better," I say. "Hurry!"

No sooner have I dispatched the kid than I see it ... a fog bank, a rock, a blur in the oceanic distance.

"Wait!" I call back to him.

"Dude...the cab's pulling out."

I squint at the watery horizon. "C'mere, son. You've got better eyes than me."

Reluctantly, he pushes his way back through the reeds.

"Dad, Peter's ad... It must have been a joke."

"What's that?" I ask. "Over there."

"Over where?"

"Over *there.*" I stab at the air. "It's a ship."

"Ya. And that's the Pacific..."

"It's headed this way."

"You don't think ..."

"Could be."

"It's not a ferry boat," Drew protests, "it's just a ..."

"Shrimper."

"Dad, there's no dock here. No place to tie up."

As the cabbie hollers our names from the road, a boat materializes in the distance, on the water line, a boat captained by a big blur of man...a man who appears to be looking for something.

STRAIGHT SHOOTER

About the Author—Zachary Michael Jack has lived and golfed in the world's great golfing meccas, including Ireland, Great Britain, and California's Monterey Peninsula. Jack learned the game from his father on the pasture course they built and designed on their Iowa Heritage Farm. A contributing writer for the WorldGolf Network and an occasional golf correspondent for the Iowa City *Press-Citizen*, the author has covered the Masters, the PGA Championship, the Ryder Cup, and the U.S. Open in addition to regular PGA Tour events, along the way interviewing major champions from Phil Mickelson to Padraig Harrington to Tom Watson. The editor of *Inside the Ropes: Sportswriters Get Their Game On*, and *Participatory Sportswriting: An Anthology*, Jack teaches undergraduate and graduate courses in sport journalism, sport literature, and sport studies at North Central College in Naperville, Illinois, where he is associate professor of English. Jack has authored or edited more than a dozen books on sport, place, and the environment.